# the BEST of FOOD

## by Marion Kane

THE TORONTO STAR

The Best of Food
Copyright © 1997 The Toronto Star

All rights reserved. No part of this
publication may be reproduced,
stored in a retrieval system, or
transmitted, in any form or by any
means, electronic, mechanical,
photocopying, recording or
otherwise, without the prior written
permission of the publisher.

Kane, Marion

ISBN 0-9690388-4-4

Published by
  The Toronto Star
  One Yonge Street,
  Toronto, Ontario
  M5E 1E6

*Design:*
  Ian Somerville
*Illustrations:*
  Raffi Anderian
*Photography:*
  Bernard Weil (front and back cover)
*Food styling:*
  Karen Boulton (front cover)

Printed and bound in Canada
by Quattro Marketing Inc.

# ACKNOWLEDGMENTS

*The sharing of good food, goodwill and good conversation is surely up there with life's true pleasures. I got my first taste of this at home.*

*My mother Ruth Schachter is an inspired, self-taught cook whose scientific background partly explains her two fortes: producing wonderful, often complicated baked goods and cleverly disguising less palatable members of the four food groups in many delectable shapes and forms.*

*My father Mel, who lives up to his family reputation as "a good little eater," put himself through medical school by working as a short order cook and imparted to me the fine art of making both French toast and salami with eggs.*

*My older daughter Esther is an accomplished cook from whom I learned much about meatless fare. Her younger sibling Ruthie is my best taster and her impeccable palate was invaluable in selecting dishes for this book.*

*Ace chef Heather Epp tested and honed most of the book's recipes with precision, diligence and imagination. Both Shelley Tanaka, meticulous cookbook editor par excellence, and the incredibly talented Toronto Star Art Director Ian Somerville, went beyond the call of duty. Karen Boulton, who has worked with me as a recipe tester and food stylist for 14 years, contributed several recipes, considerable expertise and unflagging support through thick and thin.*

Thanks to you all,

*Marion Kane*

Marion Kane

# CONTENTS

◆

*I*t has been a mission of mine since I was old enough to put whisk to bowl to discover really great recipes.

Happily, my eight years as food editor of *The Toronto Star*, Canada's biggest newspaper, have been the ideal opportunity for culinary sleuthing. I've had unique access to talented chefs, experienced recipe testers, creative cookbook authors and – my favourite source – accomplished home cooks. Now I'm delighted to share their recipes and mine in this collection that is, as Tina Turner would say, simply the best.

These dishes were love at first bite. They may have arrived at our weekly tasting session with an apology from the recipe tester such as, "I'm sorry there's only one mouthful of the Beef Beer Stew but my husband really liked it." Like the Best Brownie, they are creations that, when left on a plate in the newsroom, disappeared in seconds then elicited numerous requests for the recipe. As with the Wheat Berry Barley Risotto and Bolognese Sauce, some even inspired readers to phone me with rave reviews.

There are also recipes that my recipe testers and I created – easy, quick ideas for inexpensive fare that combined those must-have ingredients: great taste, good looks and maximum nutrition. Pasta with Greens and Beans, Spelt Salad, Risotto with Sausage and Mushrooms, Low-Fat Garlic Mashed Potatoes, Skillet Cornbread, Crème Fraîche and Tarte Tatin all fit that bill.

Finally, there are top-notch concoctions dear to my heart. Ruth's Linzertorte from my mother's dessert repertoire is, I'll vouch, the best in its genre. Likewise for two favourite fruit desserts: apple pie and applesauce. The easy-as-pie Cottage Cheese Pancakes have been a staple at family breakfasts and will be, I hope, at yours.

I urge you to try these recipes, whether it be the sweetly simple Spaghetti Casserole or more complicated Couscous with Unusual Greens. Remember, everyone has to eat and – in my opinion – anyone can cook.

Perhaps my credo will help: Cooking is a lot like riding a horse – never let the food know you're afraid of it!

◆

# Appetizers, Soups and Salads

# CRAB PUFFS

Years ago, Karen Boulton, *Toronto Star* recipe tester and amazing cook, shared this recipe for a clever, quick appetizer. Make a double batch and freeze some, or use any leftover water chestnuts in a salad or stir-fry.

*4.23-oz (120 g) can crab meat, drained*

*¾ cup (175 mL) shredded Swiss cheese (3 oz/90 g)*

*1 green onion, chopped*

*⅓ cup (75 mL) mayonnaise*

*1 clove garlic, finely chopped*

*Pinch curry powder*

*⅓ cup (75 mL) finely chopped water chestnuts*

*212 g package Pillsbury Butterflake Dinner Rolls*

In bowl, combine crab, cheese, green onion, mayonnaise, garlic, curry powder and water chestnuts.

Separate each dinner roll by pulling it in half horizontally. Place on lightly greased baking sheet. Top each biscuit with 1 tbsp (15 mL) crab mixture.

Bake in preheated 375 F (190 C) oven 20 minutes or until lightly browned.

*Makes 20 puffs.*

# A Brie Trio

*8 oz (250 g) round Brie cheese*

## Pecan Chutney:

*¼ cup (50 mL) peach or other fruit chutney*

*2 tbsp (25 mL) chopped pecans*

Spread chutney over entire surface of cheese. Sprinkle with pecans.

Bake in preheated 400 F (200 C) oven 10 to 15 minutes or until cheese is soft in centre. Let stand 5 minutes before serving.

## Caramelized Pear:

*½ pear, cored and thinly sliced*

*2 tsp (10 mL) brown sugar*

*1 tbsp (15 mL) chopped walnuts*

Place pear slices in overlapping concentric circles to cover top of Brie. Sprinkle with brown sugar and top with walnuts.

Bake in preheated 400 F (200 C) oven 10 to 15 minutes, or until soft in centre. Let stand 5 minutes before serving.

## Dried Tomato Basil:

*¼ cup (50 mL) chopped dried tomatoes (oil-packed)*

*2 tbsp (25 mL) chopped fresh basil*

*1 clove garlic, finely chopped*

*Pinch freshly ground black pepper*

In small bowl, combine tomatoes, basil, garlic and pepper. Spread over entire surface of cheese, pressing in gently. Serve cold.

*Each version makes 4 to 6 servings.*

## Brie in Puff Pastry

Top 8-oz (250 g) round Brie with layer of sliced almonds. Wrap in two or three sheets of phyllo pastry, brush with olive oil and bake at 400 F (200 C) 10 to 15 minutes or until pastry is golden-brown. Let stand 5 minutes before serving.

*This nifty appetizer with its three variations is excellent served with crackers or a sliced French stick.*

# BRUSCHETTA

*T*his always popular munchie is a great way to savour homegrown tomatoes. You could top the untoasted bread with the goat cheese, then with the tomato mixture and Parmesan and bake the bruschetta for about 10 minutes at 350 F (180 C). You could also substitute Monterey Jack or mozzarella for the goat's cheese. Of couse, you could omit the cheese altogether. A few hot pepper flakes added to the tomato mixture is also a tasty variation.

*1 lb (500 g) ripe plum tomatoes, chopped (2 cups/500 mL)*

*1 clove garlic, finely chopped*

*¼ cup (50 mL) chopped fresh basil*

*2 tbsp (25 mL) olive oil*

*¼ tsp (1 mL) salt*

*¼ tsp (1 mL) freshly ground black pepper*

*2 long Italian crusty rolls or 1 French stick*

*5 oz (150 g) soft goat cheese*

*2 tbsp (25 mL) freshly grated Parmesan cheese*

In bowl, combine tomatoes, garlic, basil, oil, salt and pepper. Slice rolls diagonally to make 16 slices 1 inch (2.5 cm) thick. Place on baking sheet.

Toast under broiler or on barbecue about 5 minutes or until just golden, turning once.

Spread goat cheese over one side of each slice. Top each with tomato mixture and sprinkle with Parmesan.

*Makes 8 servings.*

# FUTURE BAKERY'S BORSCHT

½ cup (125 mL) dried lima beans (3 oz/90 g)

2 lb (1 kg) beets, peeled and chopped (about 6 medium)

Half a small cabbage, shredded

2 onions, chopped

2 large carrots, chopped

1 stalk celery, sliced

1 leek, white only, sliced

2 cloves garlic, finely chopped

2 cups (500 mL) beef, chicken or vegetable stock

4 cups (1 L) water

1 tbsp (15 mL) white vinegar

2 tbsp (25 mL) chopped fresh dill, or 1 tsp (5 mL) dried

½ tsp (2 mL) caraway seeds

¼ tsp (1 mL) freshly ground black pepper

1 bay leaf

1 tsp (5 mL) salt

½ cup (125 mL) sour cream

1 tbsp (15 mL) all-purpose flour

Soak beans in plenty of cold water overnight; drain.

In large saucepan, combine beets, cabbage, onions, carrots, celery, leek, garlic and beans. Add stock and water. Place over medium-high heat.

Just before soup comes to a boil, add vinegar. Bring just to a boil, reduce heat and simmer about 1½ hours.

Add dill, caraway seeds, pepper, bay leaf and salt. Simmer 30 minutes.

In small bowl, stir together sour cream and flour. Add to soup and simmer 5 minutes. Taste and adjust seasoning. Discard bay leaf before serving.

*Makes 10 to 12 servings.*

The recipe they use at Future Bakery, that burgeoning Metro chain specializing in rib-hugging fare, makes 70 litres of this at a time, but we reduced the recipe to come up with a good facsimile. You could use kidney or white pea beans instead of lima beans. You could also use a 19-oz (540 mL) can of your favourite beans instead of dried beans; add them along with the spices. It is imperative to add the vinegar before the soup comes to the boil; if it's added too late or the heat's too high, the soup will turn from red to white. Meat fans could add a hunk of stewing beef along with the veggies at the initial cooking stage.

# IN-A-MO' GAZPACHO

*One of my recipe testers, Heather Trim, came up with this super version of a cold summer soup. You can vary the texture by chopping the veggies more or less finely. You could also add some chopped cucumber and green onion for garnish at the end.*

*2 large ripe tomatoes, cut in chunks*

*1 sweet yellow, red or green pepper, cut in chunks*

*1 English cucumber or 2 field cucumbers, seeded and cut in chunks*

*2 cloves garlic, finely chopped*

*6 cups (1.5 L) vegetable cocktail or tomato juice*

*4 green onions, chopped*

*¼ cup (50 mL) red wine vinegar*

*½ tsp (2 mL) hot pepper sauce, or to taste*

*Salt and freshly ground black pepper to taste*

*Croutons, homemade or storebought (optional)*

In food processor or blender, combine tomatoes, sweet pepper, cucumber and garlic. Pulse with on/off motion until evenly and coarsely chopped but not puréed. Transfer to large bowl.

Add vegetable juice, green onions, vinegar, hot pepper sauce, salt and pepper. Refrigerate at least 1 hour. Serve cold garnished with croutons (if using, see page 55).

*Makes 8 servings.*

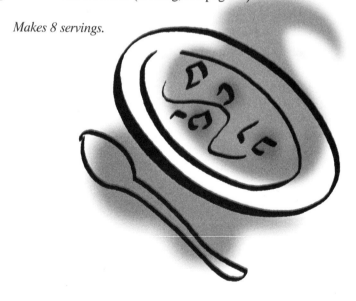

# Wheat Berry Salad

## Salad:

| |
|---|
| 1 cup (250 mL) dried wheat berries |
| 1 cup (250 mL) cooked corn kernels |
| 1 cup (250 mL) seeded and chopped cucumber or sweet green pepper |
| 1 sweet red pepper, chopped |
| ½ cup (125 mL) chopped fresh coriander or parsley |
| 4 green onions, chopped |

## Dressing:

| |
|---|
| 2 tbsp (25 mL) lemon juice |
| 2 tbsp (25 mL) olive oil |
| ½ tsp (2 mL) hot pepper sauce, or to taste |
| ½ tsp (2 mL) Dijon or honey mustard |
| Salt and freshly ground black pepper to taste |

Rinse wheat berries. Place in bowl and cover with cold water. Soak at least 6 hours or overnight. Drain well.

Place wheat berries in large saucepan with cold water to cover by at least a couple of inches. Bring to a boil, reduce heat and simmer over very low heat 1½ hours or until tender but not soft. Drain and rinse.

In large bowl, combine wheat berries, corn, cucumber, red pepper, coriander and green onions.

In separate bowl, whisk together lemon juice, olive oil, hot pepper sauce, mustard, salt and pepper. Pour dressing over salad and toss well. Serve on bed of lettuce.

*Makes 4 to 6 servings.*

*I* got this idea – and pointers on how to cook with wheat berries – from top Toronto chef/restaurateur Mark McEwan. Sold in most health-food and bulk-food stores, wheat berries are unhulled wheat kernels (either the hard or soft variety could be used in this recipe). As well as being extremely high in fibre with virtually no fat, they are tops for both taste and texture. The berries require soaking and long cooking but are well worth the effort. I like to keep a stash of cooked berries in my fridge to serve as a carbo sidekick or to toss with a favourite salad dressing along with whatever fresh veggies I have on hand.

# Spelt Salad

*Giuliano Bugialli is one of my favourite foodies. Blessed with a great sense of humour, this ace cook and instructor (based in New York, he also has a cooking school in his native Florence) always peppers his topnotch demos with great anecdotes and lots of interesting information. He recently shared his new appreciation of spelt – an ancient wheat grain that is both delicious and packed with nutrients. I changed his recipe to make it vegetarian (removed the pancetta) and made a few other adaptations. For a dinner party, you could serve this on a bed of radicchio. Substitute 19 oz (540 mL) canned beans for the dried ones used here; just drain and rinse them before adding them to the cooked spelt.*

*1 cup (250 mL) dried pinto or kidney beans (8 oz/250 g), soaked overnight, drained*

*1 cup (250 mL) spelt kernels (8 oz/250 g), soaked overnight, drained*

*½ tsp (2 mL) salt*

*12 oz (375 g) small carrots, sliced*

*12 oz (375 g) green or yellow wax beans, cut in 2-inch (5 cm) lengths*

*½ cup (125 mL) olive oil*

*3 cloves garlic, finely chopped*

*Pinch hot pepper flakes*

*Salt and freshly ground black pepper to taste*

*1 cup (250 mL) coarsely chopped fresh basil leaves*

In large saucepan, cover soaked beans with fresh water. Bring to a boil, reduce heat and simmer about 50 minutes or until beans are tender but still holding their shape. Drain.

In same saucepan, cover soaked spelt kernels with cold water. Bring to a boil, reduce heat and simmer 30 minutes. Add cooked pinto beans and salt. Simmer 10 minutes to allow flavours to blend. Drain and place in large serving bowl.

In medium saucepan of boiling salted water, cook carrots and green beans about 4 minutes or until just tender. Drain and rinse with cold water. Add to salad.

In small skillet over medium heat, combine oil, garlic and hot pepper flakes. Heat about 2 minutes, without browning garlic. Pour over salad. Season with salt and pepper and toss well. Refrigerate. Toss in basil just before serving.

*Makes 10 to 12 servings.*

# OLD-FASHIONED POTATO SALAD

*3 lb (1.5 kg) potatoes, scrubbed and cubed*

*¼ cup (50 mL) dill pickle juice*

*⅔ cup (150 mL) mayonnaise*

*⅓ cup (75 mL) Miracle Whip*

*Salt and freshly ground black pepper to taste*

*2 hard-boiled eggs, chopped*

*1 large dill pickle, chopped*

*2 stalks celery, chopped*

*2 tbsp (25 mL) chopped fresh parsley*

*4 green onions, chopped*

In saucepan, cover potatoes with plenty of water and boil 8 to 10 minutes or until tender. Drain and transfer to large bowl. While potatoes are still hot, stir in pickle juice; cool.

In small bowl, combine mayonnaise, Miracle Whip, salt and pepper. Add to potatoes along with eggs, pickle, celery, parsley and green onions. (For a moister salad, add a little water.) Toss gently.

*Makes 6 to 8 servings.*

## Low-fat Tofu Dressing

In food processor, purée 8 oz (250 g) drained soft tofu (about 1¼ cups (300 mL), ⅓ cup (75 mL) low-fat mayonnaise, ⅓ cup (75 mL) low-fat plain yogurt, 1 tbsp (15 mL) cider vinegar, 3 tbsp (45 mL) Dijon mustard, 2 finely chopped cloves garlic (optional) and salt and pepper to taste.

*Still my favourite in its genre, this creamy summer standby could easily be doubled for a crowd. For a low-fat version, omit the dill pickle juice, substitute 6 chopped egg whites for the whole eggs and make our Low-fat Tofu Dressing.*

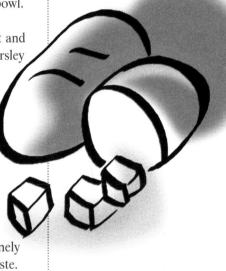

# Caesar Dressing for the '90s

This excellent low-fat dressing made with cooked eggs and roasted garlic is enough for two heads of Romaine lettuce and about 2 cups (500 mL) croutons (page 55). It came from Pino Posteraro, a talented chef who was once the owner of Yorkville restaurant, Borgo Antico. You could halve the recipe or store any leftovers in the fridge for up to one week.

*3 hard-boiled egg yolks*

*4 large roasted garlic cloves (page 98)*

*2 tbsp (25 mL) horseradish*

*4 tsp (20 mL) Dijon mustard*

*1 anchovy*

*1 tbsp (15 mL) capers*

*Salt and freshly ground black pepper to taste*

*Dash hot pepper sauce (optional)*

*1½ cups (375 mL) plain low-fat yogurt*

*¼ cup (50 mL) freshly grated Parmesan cheese*

In blender or food processor, combine egg yolks, garlic, horseradish, mustard, anchovy, capers, salt, pepper, hot pepper sauce (if using) and ½ cup (125 mL) plain yogurt. Transfer to bowl.

Stir in remaining yogurt and Parmesan.

*Makes about 1½ cups (375 mL).*

## Old-fashioned Caesar Dressing

In blender or food processor, combine 2 finely chopped cloves garlic, 3 anchovies, 1 tsp (5 mL) granulated sugar, 1 tsp (5 mL) Dijon mustard, ¼ cup (50 mL) wine vinegar, ½ tsp (2 mL) Worcestershire sauce, 1 egg, 2 tbsp (25 mL) chopped fresh parsley, ¼ tsp (1 mL) freshly ground black pepper, ¼ cup (50 mL) freshly grated Parmesan cheese and ¾ cup (175 mL) olive oil. Makes about 1¼ cups (300 mL).

# *Pasta*

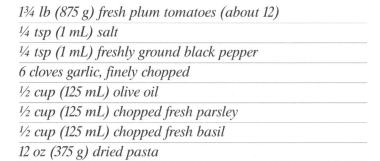

# PASTA WITH OVEN-ROASTED TOMATO SAUCE

*This fabulous idea for a robust sauce that highlights those flavour-packed plum tomatoes is from Foodland Ontario. Use locally grown tomatoes during the summer for this; they have fabulous taste and firm texture.*

*1¾ lb (875 g) fresh plum tomatoes (about 12)*

*¼ tsp (1 mL) salt*

*¼ tsp (1 mL) freshly ground black pepper*

*6 cloves garlic, finely chopped*

*½ cup (125 mL) olive oil*

*½ cup (125 mL) chopped fresh parsley*

*½ cup (125 mL) chopped fresh basil*

*12 oz (375 g) dried pasta*

*Freshly grated Parmesan cheese*

Cut tomatoes in half lengthwise. Place cut side up in 13 x 9-inch (3 L) baking dish. Sprinkle with salt and pepper.

In small bowl, combine garlic, ¼ cup (50 mL) oil and ¼ cup (50 mL) parsley. Spread over tomatoes.

Bake in preheated 425 F (220 C) oven about 70 minutes or until tops are slightly charred. Cool 15 minutes.

Squeeze tomato pulp into bowl, discarding skins. Coarsely mash or chop pulp. Stir in remaining oil, parsley and basil.

Meanwhile, cook pasta in large saucepan of boiling salted water until just tender. Drain.

Toss hot cooked pasta with sauce. Sprinkle with Parmesan.

*Makes 4 to 6 servings.*

# BIBA'S RICOTTA GNOCCHI

*1 lb (500 g) ricotta cheese*

*1 to 1½ cups (250 to 375 mL) all-purpose flour*

In large bowl, combine ricotta and 1 cup (250 mL) flour. Gradually stir in enough remaining flour to form a soft, not sticky, dough.

Break off a piece of dough about the size of an egg. On lightly floured work surface, using hands, roll dough into long log about the diameter of a finger. Cut into ½-inch (1 cm) pieces. Place on baking sheet lined with tea towel. Repeat with remaining dough. Keep refrigerated until ready to cook (or freeze and cook directly from frozen state).

In large saucepan of boiling salted water, cook gnocchi 2 to 3 minutes or until they rise to the surface. Remove with slotted spoon and transfer to warm dish.

*Makes 4 to 6 servings.*

## Biba's Quickie Tomato Sauce

Purée 28-oz (796 mL) can tomatoes, drained. Simmer for about 10 minutes to thicken slightly. Add 1 tbsp (15 mL) butter and salt and freshly ground black pepper to taste.

*A* super version of a recipe from Biba Caggiano's cookbook, *Modern Italian Cooking*. We ran this when Caggiano, the engaging and accomplished California-based chef/restaurateur and TV cooking-show host, was in town. Serve it with Biba's Quickie Tomato Sauce or your favourite tomato sauce, and sprinkle with Parmesan cheese. You could use low-fat ricotta if desired.

# IN-THE-RAW HARLOT'S PASTA

*This fabulous uncooked tomato sauce is a version of the traditional Pasta Puttanesca which, translated, means Whore's Pasta. If you are using larger round tomatoes, peel and seed them before chopping (page 61). As a sauce for pasta, this can be served heated or at room temperature. It would also make a great salsa. All kinds of other ingredients can also be added. Try adding 8 oz (250 g) cubed mozzarella cheese, ½ cup (125 mL) small black olives or chopped red onion, ¼ cup (50 mL) chopped fresh parsley, basil, oregano or chives, 1 tbsp (15 mL) finely chopped anchovies or capers, 2 tbsp (25 mL) toasted pine nuts or a pinch of hot pepper flakes.*

| |
|---|
| *2 lb (1 kg) fresh plum tomatoes, coarsely chopped* |
| *¼ cup (50 mL) olive oil* |
| *1 tbsp (15 mL) balsamic vinegar* |
| *1 clove garlic, finely chopped* |
| *¼ cup (50 mL) chopped fresh basil* |
| *½ tsp (2 mL) salt* |
| *½ tsp (2 mL) freshly ground black pepper* |
| *1 lb (500 g) dried pasta* |

In large serving bowl, combine tomatoes, oil, vinegar, garlic, basil, salt and pepper. Let stand at room temperature 30 minutes.

Meanwhile, cook pasta in large saucepan of boiling salted water about 8 minutes or until just tender. Drain.

Toss pasta with tomato sauce.

*Makes 6 servings.*

# Penne à la Vodka

| |
|---|
| 2 tbsp (25 mL) vegetable oil |
| 1 small onion, chopped |
| 4 cloves garlic, finely chopped |
| ½ tsp (2 mL) hot pepper flakes |
| 28-oz (796 mL) can tomatoes, undrained, chopped |
| 1 cup (250 mL) whipping cream |
| ¼ cup (50 mL) vodka |
| Salt and freshly ground black pepper to taste |
| 1 lb (500 g) dried penne |
| ¼ cup (50 mL) freshly grated Parmesan cheese |
| 2 tbsp (25 mL) chopped fresh parsley |

Heat oil in large skillet or saucepan over medium heat. Stir in onion, garlic and hot pepper flakes. Cook about 4 minutes or until softened but not browned. Stir in tomatoes and bring to a boil. Reduce heat and simmer about 10 minutes or until thickened.

Add cream, vodka, salt and pepper. Bring to a boil, reduce heat and simmer 5 minutes.

Meanwhile, cook penne in large saucepan of boiling salted water about 8 minutes or just until tender. Drain.

Stir pasta into sauce. Turn off heat and let stand on element about 5 minutes or until some of the sauce has been absorbed. Serve immediately topped with Parmesan cheese and parsley.

*Makes 4 to 6 servings.*

*Our* version of a classic that has survived at least three decades as a terrific dinner-party dish because of its magnificent taste and easy preparation. Forget the calories and enjoy! This would also be great tossed with julienned smoked salmon and/or steamed snowpeas or asparagus.

# PASTA WITH TOFU AND OLIVES

*I* got this super idea from my daughter Esther who, during the time she was a strict vegetarian, was always coming up with good ideas for meatless dishes. Tofu, when blended, is excellent for making a creamy sauce. It is important to use good-quality olives for this; canned and some bulk-store olives are either too salty or too bland. Choose Kalamata olives, often sold at deli counters or Mediterranean-neighbourhood markets. Dried tomatoes would be a flavourful lower-fat substitute for some or all of the olives. Or you could use less or even omit the olives altogether. Reconstitute them by covering them with hot water for 10 to 15 minutes or until tender but not mushy, then chop. Miso is a soybean paste; dark miso is stronger in taste than light.

| |
|---|
| *1 lb (500 g) soft tofu, drained (about 3 cups/750 mL)* |
| *2 tbsp (25 mL) olive oil* |
| *2 onions, diced* |
| *2 cups (500 mL) chopped fresh kale or spinach* |
| *1 bay leaf* |
| *1 tbsp (15 mL) chopped fresh basil, or ½ tsp (2 mL) dried* |
| *1 tbsp (15 mL) chopped fresh oregano, or ½ tsp (2 mL) dried* |
| *1 tbsp (15 mL) chopped fresh thyme, or ½ tsp (2 mL) dried* |
| *¼ cup (50 mL) light miso* |
| *⅓ cup (75 mL) black olives, pitted and chopped* |
| *⅓ cup (75 mL) green olives, pitted and chopped* |
| *1 lb (500 g) dried fettuccine, linguine or other long noodles* |
| *Freshly ground black pepper to taste* |
| *¼ cup (50 mL) chopped green onions* |

Bring small saucepan of water to a boil. Add tofu and simmer 3 minutes. Drain.

Heat oil in skillet over medium heat. Add onions, kale, bay leaf, basil, oregano and thyme. Cook, stirring occasionally, about 10 minutes or until onions are soft, reducing heat to low after 3 to 4 minutes. Discard bay leaf.

In food processor or blender, purée onion mixture with tofu and miso until smooth and creamy (for a chunkier sauce mix ingredients by hand). Stir in olives.

Meanwhile, in large saucepan of boiling salted water, cook pasta until tender but firm. Drain. Immediately toss with tofu mixture. Season with pepper. Garnish with green onions.

*Makes 4 servings.*

# LOW-FAT FETTUCCINE ALFREDO #1

*1 lb (500 g) dried fettuccine*

*1 tsp (5 mL) olive oil*

*3 cloves garlic, finely chopped*

*1 cup (250 mL) low-fat sour cream*

*¼ cup (50 mL) freshly grated Parmesan cheese*

*2 tbsp (25 mL) chopped fresh parsley*

*Salt and freshly ground black pepper to taste*

In large saucepan of boiling salted water, cook pasta until just tender. Drain.

Meanwhile, heat oil in large skillet over medium heat. Add garlic. Cook 30 seconds, without browning. Stir in sour cream and Parmesan. Bring just to a boil.

Add pasta, parsley, salt and pepper. Cook about 2 minutes or until heated through.

*Makes 4 to 6 servings.*

## LOW-FAT FETTUCCINE ALFREDO #2

*1 lb (500 g) dried fettuccine*

*1 tsp (5 mL) olive oil*

*3 cloves garlic, finely chopped*

*385 mL can evaporated skim milk*

*½ cup (125 mL) low-fat cream cheese*

*¼ cup (50 mL) freshly grated Parmesan cheese*

*Pinch grated nutmeg*

*2 tbsp (25 mL) chopped fresh parsley*

*Salt and freshly ground black pepper to taste*

In large saucepan of boiling salted water, cook pasta just until tender. Drain.

Meanwhile, heat oil in large skillet over medium heat. Add garlic. Cook 30 seconds, without browning. Stir in milk, cream cheese and Parmesan. Cook about 7 minutes or until cheese has melted and milk has just come to a boil, whisking until smooth.

Stir in pasta, nutmeg, parsley, salt and pepper. Cook about 2 minutes or until heated through.

*Makes 4 to 6 servings.*

*I*t's hard to make a creamy pasta sauce that's low in fat and tastes good, but I accepted the challenge and developed two versions that, I think, taste great. These are fabulous quick supper dishes and can be easily augmented by adding chunks of cooked chicken, canned tuna or, for a fancy meal, smoked salmon. In a pinch, the cream cheese could be omitted from #2.

# Pasta with Fresh Herbs and Gorgonzola

*U*se just the leaves, not the stems of the herbs for this robust, full-flavoured dish that's great to make at the height of fresh herb season. It has been adapted from a recipe by the International Olive Oil Council. Serve with a salad, crusty bread and a full-bodied red wine like Amarone.

| |
|---|
| ¼ cup (50 mL) chopped fresh basil |
| ¼ cup (50 mL) chopped fresh parsley |
| 2 tbsp (25 mL) chopped fresh oregano |
| 2 tbsp (25 mL) chopped fresh thyme |
| 1 lb (500 g) dried spaghetti |
| ¼ cup (50 mL) olive oil |
| 2 garlic cloves, finely chopped |
| ¼ tsp (1 mL) hot pepper flakes, or to taste |
| 1½ lb (750 g) fresh tomatoes, seeded and chopped (about 3 cups/750 mL) |
| Salt and freshly ground black pepper to taste |
| 6 oz (175 g) Gorgonzola cheese, crumbled (about ⅔ cup/150 mL) |
| Freshly grated Parmesan cheese |

In small bowl, combine basil, parsley, oregano and thyme.

In large saucepan of boiling salted water, cook spaghetti until just tender. Drain.

Meanwhile, heat oil in small skillet over medium heat. Add garlic, hot pepper flakes and half the mixed herbs. Reduce heat and simmer gently 2 to 3 minutes.

Place pasta in heated serving bowl. Top with tomatoes and uncooked herbs. Season with salt and pepper. Sprinkle Gorgonzola over top. Pour in cooked herb mixture and toss until well mixed. Serve immediately with Parmesan cheese.

*Makes 4 to 6 servings.*

# SPAGHETTI CASSEROLE

| |
|---|
| *1 lb (500 g) dried spaghetti* |
| *3 tbsp (45 mL) vegetable oil* |
| *1 onion, chopped* |
| *1 lb (500 g) lean ground beef, chicken or turkey* |
| *3 cups (750 mL) tomato sauce* |
| *Salt and freshly ground black pepper to taste* |
| *½ tsp (2 mL) dried oregano* |
| *½ tsp (2 mL) dried basil* |
| *8 oz (250 g) cream cheese, at room temperature* |
| *3 cups (750 mL) cottage cheese* |
| *½ cup (125 mL) chopped green onions* |
| *1 sweet green pepper, chopped* |
| *¼ cup (50 mL) freshly grated Parmesan cheese* |

Cook spaghetti in large saucepan of boiling salted water until almost tender. Drain. Stir in 1 tbsp (15 mL) vegetable oil to keep spaghetti from sticking together.

In large skillet or saucepan, heat remaining 2 tbsp (25 mL) oil over medium-high heat. Add onion and cook 3 minutes or until soft. Add ground meat and cook until meat is browned, about 5 minutes. Drain off excess fat. Stir in tomato sauce, salt, pepper, oregano and basil.

In large bowl, beat cream cheese with wooden spoon until smooth. Beat in cottage cheese. Stir in green onions and green pepper.

Spread half the spaghetti over bottom of lightly greased 13 x 9-inch (3 L) baking dish. Spoon over half the cheese mixture and half the meat sauce. Repeat layers. Sprinkle with Parmesan.

Bake, uncovered, in 350 F (180 C) oven 35 to 45 minutes or until bubbly. Let stand 15 minutes before serving.

*Makes 8 to 10 servings.*

◆

*T*his is for anyone who loves lasagna but can't be bothered with all those fiddly layers. The recipe calls for spaghetti (although any pasta shape will do), and it is literally child's play to prepare (a friend's youngster made it for a school cooking project). Easily made ahead, it's a great family dish served with a green salad or steamed veggies. Vegetarians could substitute a 19-oz (540 mL) can of beans for the ground meat — just add them with the tomato sauce.
You could also add 1 cup (250 mL) corn kernels and/or hot pepper sauce. Use low-fat cottage cheese and cream cheese if you wish and, if you like lots of sauce, add an extra cup of tomato sauce.

◆

# Upscale Macaroni and Cheese

*A*sk the butcher to cut a thick piece of ham, or use pre-cut ham steaks for this gourmet version of an old favourite. I developed this for a feature on macaroni and cheese and discovered that using goat cheese in the mixture added wondrous flavour. I prefer to use white rather than orange Cheddar for this. Bound to be a hit with everyone, this needs only a salad and good bread to round out a meal that could be everyday fare or fancy enough for guests.

|  |
| --- |
| 3 tbsp (45 mL) butter |
| 2 cloves garlic, finely chopped |
| 3 tbsp (45 mL) all-purpose flour |
| 2½ cups (625 mL) milk |
| ½ tsp (2 mL) salt |
| Pinch grated nutmeg |
| Pinch cayenne pepper |
| 2½ cups (625 mL) shredded Cheddar cheese (10 oz/300 g) |
| 10 oz (300 g) soft goat cheese |
| 1 lb (500 g) short dried pasta (e.g., macaroni, penne, fusilli or rotini) |
| 12 oz (375 g) smoked ham, cubed |
| 2 tbsp (25 mL) dry breadcrumbs |
| 2 tbsp (25 mL) freshly grated Parmesan cheese |

Melt butter in small, heavy-bottomed saucepan over medium heat. Add garlic and cook 30 seconds without browning. Add flour and cook 1 minute, stirring constantly. Gradually whisk in milk until smooth. Add salt, nutmeg and cayenne. Bring to a boil, slowly, over medium heat, stirring occasionally, until thickened, about 15 minutes. Stir in Cheddar and goat cheeses until melted. Remove from heat.

Meanwhile, in large saucepan of boiling salted water, cook pasta about 8 minutes or until just tender. Drain.

In large bowl, combine cheese sauce, pasta and ham. Pour into shallow buttered 12-cup (3 L) casserole dish.

In small bowl, combine breadcrumbs and Parmesan. Sprinkle over pasta. Bake in preheated 350 F (180 C) oven about 30 minutes or until bubbling. Place under broiler about 2 minutes to brown topping, if desired.

*Makes 6 servings.*

# PASTA WITH BEANS AND GREENS

*2 cups (500 mL) short dried pasta
(e.g. bow-ties, fusilli or penne)*

*2 tbsp (25 mL) olive oil*

*3 cloves garlic, finely chopped*

*1 bunch green onions, chopped*

*10 oz (300 g) fresh spinach, chopped*

*19-oz (540 mL) can Italian stewed tomatoes,
undrained, chopped*

*19-oz (540 mL) can Romano, cannellini
or other beans, drained and rinsed*

*1 tbsp (15 mL) balsamic vinegar*

*½ tsp (2 mL) salt*

*¼ tsp (1 mL) freshly ground black pepper*

Cook pasta in large saucepan of boiling salted water about 8 minutes or until tender. Drain.

Meanwhile, heat oil in large skillet. Add garlic and green onions. Cook, stirring occasionally, about 4 minutes or until softened. Stir in spinach, tossing to coat with oil. Add tomatoes. Cook 5 minutes or until spinach has wilted.

Stir in beans, cooked pasta, vinegar, salt and pepper. Cook about 5 minutes or until heated through.

*Makes 6 servings.*

*A* winner, though I say so myself. You could use other canned beans such as chickpeas, kidney beans or fava beans in this amazingly tasty, quick and inexpensive meatless dish. In season, this would be out of this world made with fresh soy, cranberry or fava beans, simply removed from the pods and boiled for about 30 minutes. The flavoured canned tomatoes (Mexican, Italian etc.) are ideal for this dish. A superb weeknight family meal, a great dinner-party dish and a fabulous potluck or buffet offering.

# SPICY PASTA WITH LENTILS

*You could use a 19-oz (540 mL) can of chickpeas or other beans in this tasty meatless main dish. Just drain and rinse them, then add to the skillet as you would the lentils. The larger green lentils will require at least twice as much cooking time as the smaller red or brown ones used here.*

*2½ cups (625 mL) water*

*1 cup (250 mL) red or brown dried lentils, rinsed*

*2 cups (500 mL) short dried pasta (e.g., bow-ties or shells)*

*1 tbsp (15 mL) olive oil*

*1 small onion, chopped*

*1 small stalk celery, chopped*

*1 carrot, peeled and grated*

*6 mushrooms, chopped*

*1 clove garlic, finely chopped*

*28-oz (796 mL) can tomatoes, undrained, chopped*

*1 bay leaf*

*Dash hot pepper sauce*

*½ tsp (2 mL) salt*

*½ tsp (2 mL) freshly ground black pepper*

*2 tbsp (25 mL) balsamic vinegar*

*Freshly grated Parmesan cheese*

Bring water to a boil in saucepan. Stir in lentils and return to a boil. Reduce heat and simmer 15 minutes. Drain.

Cook pasta in large saucepan of boiling salted water about 5 minutes or until just tender. Drain.

Meanwhile, heat oil in large skillet over medium heat. Add onion, celery, carrot, mushrooms and garlic. Cook, stirring, about 5 minutes or until vegetables have softened. Stir in tomatoes, lentils, bay leaf, hot pepper sauce, salt and pepper. Bring to a boil and simmer about 25 minutes or until sauce has thickened. Discard bay leaf.

In food processor, purée about 1 cup (250 mL) lentil mixture if desired. Return to skillet. Stir in vinegar and pasta. Serve topped with Parmesan.

*Makes 4 servings.*

# Pasta e Fagioli

3 tbsp (45 mL) olive oil

2 cloves garlic, finely chopped

½ small onion, finely chopped

½ small carrot, peeled and finely chopped

½ stalk celery, finely chopped

¼ tsp (1 mL) hot pepper flakes

4 cups (1 L) vegetable or chicken stock

28-oz (796 mL) can tomatoes, undrained, chopped

19-oz (540 mL) can chickpeas, drained and rinsed

19-oz (540 mL) can Romano beans, drained and rinsed

19-oz (540 mL) can cannellini beans, drained and rinsed

8 oz (250 g) short dried pasta
(e.g., shells, bow-ties, penne)

Salt and freshly ground black pepper to taste

Freshly grated Parmesan cheese

Heat oil in large saucepan over medium heat. Add garlic, onion, carrot, celery and hot pepper flakes. Cook 3 minutes or until tender, but do not brown. Add stock and tomatoes. Bring to a boil, reduce heat and simmer, partially covered, 20 minutes. Stir in chickpeas and beans. Simmer 10 minutes, stirring frequently.

In food processor, purée 2 cups (500 mL) bean mixture. Return to saucepan.

Return to boil and stir in pasta. Simmer over low heat about 8 minutes, stirring frequently, until pasta is just tender. Add salt and pepper.

Serve sprinkled with Parmesan.

*Makes 6 servings.*

This cross between a soup and a stew makes a great one-pot meatless meal. An Italian staple, this is best topped with the top-quality Parmesan called Parmigiano Reggiano, available at most Italian food shops and some supermarkets. Wrap the whole piece well in foil or two layers of plastic wrap and store in the fridge. Grate just before using. If you find this dish too thick (leftovers tend to thicken after being stored in the fridge), just add more stock or water. You can use almost any kind of beans, or you might prefer to use just one kind. If you are using home-cooked dried beans, substitute about 2 cups (500 mL) cooked beans (¾ cup/175 mL dried) for each can.

A nifty way to chop canned tomatoes is to cut them, still in the can, with a pair of kitchen scissors.

# BOLOGNESE SAUCE

| | |
|---|---|
| 2 tbsp (25 mL) vegetable oil | |
| 1 small onion, chopped | |
| 3 cloves garlic, finely chopped | |
| 2 carrots, peeled and chopped | |
| 1 stalk celery, chopped | |
| 1½ lb (750 g) lean ground beef | |
| 1 tsp (5 mL) salt | |
| 1 cup (250 mL) dry white wine | |
| ½ cup (125 mL) milk | |
| Two 28-oz (796 mL) cans tomatoes, undrained, chopped | |
| ¼ cup (50 mL) chopped fresh basil or 1 tbsp (15 mL) dried | |
| 1 tbsp (15 mL) chopped fresh oregano or 1 tsp (5 mL) dried | |
| Freshly ground black pepper to taste | |

*My* source for the unusual but key initial step of this recipe – cooking most of the ingredients in white wine and then milk before simmering them with the tomatoes – is brilliant Italian cook and author Marcella Hazan. I adapted the idea and came up with a meat sauce for pasta that is just bursting with flavour. Try it and you'll wonder where this recipe has been all your life. It makes enough for 1 lb (500 g) pasta but is also great whenever you need a meat sauce. I like to serve it over a wedge of baked winter squash sprinkled with freshly grated Parmesan. Keep some in the freezer, and you'll never be stuck for a quick meal the whole family will love.

Heat oil in large saucepan over medium heat. Add onion and cook, stirring occasionally, about 4 minutes or until soft. Stir in garlic, carrots and celery. Cook about 2 minutes. Increase heat to high. Add ground beef and salt, stirring to break up lumps. Cook about 5 minutes or until meat is no longer pink. Stir in wine. Bring to a boil, reduce heat and simmer about 7 minutes or until wine has almost evaporated. Stir in milk and bring to a boil. Reduce heat and simmer about 5 minutes or until milk has almost evaporated. Add tomatoes, basil, oregano and pepper. Bring to a boil, reduce heat and simmer, uncovered or partially covered, about 3½ hours or until thick, stirring occasionally and adding a little water or white wine if sauce becomes dry.

*Makes 6 to 8 servings.*

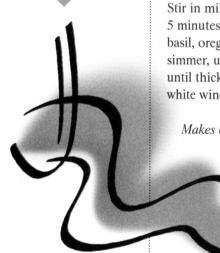

# PEANUT SAUCE

*½ cup (125 mL) peanut butter*

*¼ cup (50 mL) soy sauce*

*¼ cup (50 mL) cider vinegar or rice vinegar*

*¼ cup (50 mL) granulated sugar*

*2 tbsp (25 mL) finely chopped fresh ginger root*

*5 cloves garlic, finely chopped*

*1 tbsp (15 mL) dark sesame oil*

*1 tsp (5 mL) hot pepper flakes or hot pepper sauce*

*1 large bunch fresh coriander, coarsely chopped*

In food processor or blender, combine peanut butter, soy sauce, vinegar, sugar, ginger, garlic, sesame oil and hot pepper flakes. Process until fairly smooth. Add coriander. Pulse with on/off motion just until coriander is finely chopped.

*Makes 1½ cups (375 mL).*

*T*his versatile sauce developed by Heather Epp is wonderful on hot or cold noodles, as a dipping sauce for chicken or beef satays, or to drizzle over grilled vegetables. It makes enough for 1½ lb (750 g) noodles and is great for serving a crowd at a buffet. You can use chunky or smooth peanut butter.

# THAI SPICY NOODLES

Called pad thai, this fabulous combination of tastes and textures has made it onto the menus of all kinds of restaurants around town – and small wonder. We developed this version after many tries and, in my opinion, it's superb. Tamarind (usually sold as a paste made from this sweet-and-sour tropical fruit), fish sauce, chili paste and fried tofu are available in Chinese or Thai food stores. In a pinch you could use lemon juice instead of lime juice. The white and barely opaque rice noodles come in different widths and are sometimes called rice sticks. You can make this more or less hot by varying the amount of chili paste; we like the sambal oelek brand (with the rooster on the jar) sold in all Chinatowns.

| |
|---|
| 227 g package ¼-inch (.5 cm) wide rice noodles |
| 3 tbsp (45 mL) preserved tamarind |
| ¼ cup (50 mL) boiling water |
| ¼ cup (50 mL) ketchup |
| ¼ cup (50 mL) fish sauce |
| 2 tbsp (25 mL) lime juice |
| 1 tbsp (15 mL) soy sauce |
| 1 tbsp (15 mL) granulated sugar |
| 2 tsp (10 mL) hot Oriental chili paste |
| ¼ cup (50 mL) vegetable oil |
| 3 cloves garlic, finely chopped |
| 8 oz (250 g) boneless, skinless chicken breast, cut in ½-inch (1 cm) cubes |
| 8 oz (250 g) shrimp, peeled and deveined |
| 4 oz (125 g) fried tofu, cut in ½-inch (1 cm) cubes |
| 2 eggs, beaten |
| 3 cups (750 mL) bean sprouts |
| ½ cup (125 mL) unsalted peanuts, coarsely chopped (2 oz/60 g) |
| 3 green onions, chopped |
| ½ cup (125 mL) fresh coriander or parsley leaves |

Place rice noodles in large bowl, cover with cold water and let stand about 20 minutes. Drain.

In small bowl, combine tamarind and boiling water, stirring to soften; let cool. Press tamarind through sieve, discarding seeds. You should have about 2 tbsp (25 mL) tamarind purée.

In separate bowl, combine tamarind, ketchup, fish sauce, lime juice, soy sauce, sugar and chili paste, stirring until smooth.

Heat oil in wok over high heat until very hot. Add garlic, chicken, shrimp and tofu. Cook, stirring constantly, about 2 minutes or until chicken is no longer pink inside. Make a well in centre. Add egg and let set slightly, then stir to scramble. Add noodles, bean sprouts and sauce. Stir-fry about 5 minutes or until noodles have softened and all ingredients are combined and well coated with sauce.

Place on large platter. Garnish with peanuts, green onions and fresh coriander leaves.

*Makes 4 servings.*

# ORIENTAL CHICKEN NOODLE SALAD

*⅓ cup (75 mL) red wine vinegar*

*⅓ cup (75 mL) dark sesame oil*

*¼ cup (50 mL) soy sauce*

*2 tbsp (25 mL) light miso (page 20)*
*or 1 tbsp (15 mL) dark miso (optional)*

*1 tbsp (15 mL) granulated sugar*

*1 tbsp (15 mL) finely chopped fresh ginger root*

*½ tsp (2 mL) hot Oriental chili paste*
*or hot pepper sauce, or to taste*

*12 oz (375 g) dried Chinese egg noodle nests or linguine*

*2 cups (500 mL) cubed cooked chicken*

*2 cups (500 mL) bean sprouts, or peeled and*
*seeded cucumber, cut in strips*

*4 cups (1 L) shredded iceberg lettuce (½ head)*

*4 fresh plum tomatoes, chopped*

*¼ cup (50 mL) chopped fresh coriander or parsley*

*¼ cup (50 mL) chopped roasted peanuts*

In small bowl, whisk together vinegar, oil, soy sauce, miso (if using), sugar, ginger and chili paste.

In large saucepan of boiling salted water, cook noodles about 4 minutes (8 minutes if using linguine).  Drain.

Toss noodles in large bowl with half of sauce. At this point ingredients can be refrigerated up to 4 hours.

To serve, toss chicken, bean sprouts, lettuce, tomatoes and remaining sauce with noodles. Garnish with coriander and peanuts.

*Makes 6 servings.*

*I* created this yummy salad a few years ago when I was having my kitchen renovated and was cooking in reduced circumstances. Quick and easy to prepare, it has an excellent contrast of tastes and textures and makes a great potluck offering or barbecue side dish. The best noodles for this are the fettuccine-shaped Chinese dried egg noodles usually sold in nest shapes, but fresh or dried Italian pasta, especially linguine or fettuccine, also works well.

# Penne with Sausage

A super, quick pasta dish from Al Carbone of Kit Kat Italian Bar & Grill near SkyDome, who says this is a favourite of Dan Aykroyd, a restaurant regular. Carbone uses sausages made specially for him, but many places, even supermarkets, sell good ones these days. If you are using commercial tomato sauce, choose a good-quality brand such as Classico.

Serve this with crusty bread, robust red wine and a green salad. You could substitute leftover chicken, turkey or other meat for the sausage if you wish. Again, use this recipe as a guide depending on your whim, the season or the contents of your fridge.

*4 fresh spicy Italian sausages*

*1 clove garlic, finely chopped*

*¼ cup (50 mL) dry white wine*

*1 tsp (5 mL) olive oil*

*3 cups (750 mL) tomato sauce*

*¼ cup (50 mL) chopped fresh basil*

*1 lb (500 g) dried penne or other short pasta*

*¼ cup (50 mL) freshly grated Parmesan cheese*

In large skillet, over medium-high heat, cook sausages about 5 minutes or until browned. Slice into rounds ¼ inch (5 mm) thick. Return to skillet and cook about 7 minutes or until no longer pink. Stir in garlic and cook 1 minute or until just golden. Add wine, stirring to scrape up brown bits from skillet. Simmer 5 minutes or until liquid has almost been absorbed. Add olive oil and tomato sauce. Bring to a boil, reduce heat and simmer about 5 minutes or until slightly thickened. Stir in basil.

Meanwhile, in large saucepan of boiling salted water, cook penne until just tender. Drain.

In large bowl, toss pasta with sauce. Top with Parmesan.

*Makes 4 servings.*

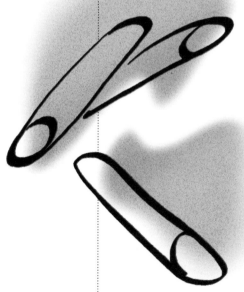

# *Meatless Main Courses*

# ORANGE TERIYAKI TOFU

*This amazingly tasty creation comes from Eta Brand, who once owned and operated a Toronto cooking school. I am a fan of tofu – a good, low-fat, meatless source of protein – as long as it's gussied up with plenty of flavourful ingredients as it definitely is here. Firm tofu, a must for this version, is sold in most health-food stores and many supermarkets. Weather permitting, barbecuing is my favoured way of cooking this.*

| |
|---|
| *1 lb (500 g) firm tofu (not extra-firm)* |
| *¼ cup (50 mL) tamari sauce or soy sauce* |
| *3 tbsp (45 mL) rice vinegar* |
| *3 tbsp (45 mL) maple syrup* |
| *½ cup (125 mL) orange juice* |
| *2 tsp (10 mL) finely grated orange rind* |
| *1 tsp (5 mL) finely chopped fresh ginger root* |
| *2 cloves garlic, finely chopped* |
| *¼ tsp (1 mL) dry mustard* |
| *Chopped fresh coriander or parsley* |

Cut tofu into bite-sized squares or slices ½ inch (1 cm) thick. Place in shallow baking dish or casserole.

In small bowl, combine tamari, vinegar, maple syrup, orange juice, orange rind, ginger, garlic and mustard. Pour over tofu. Marinate at least 1 hour or up to 24 hours.

Pour marinade into measuring cup. Return ½ cup (125 mL) to tofu in baking dish and discard the rest.

Bake in preheated 375 F (190 C) oven about 1 hour, gently stirring and basting every 20 minutes. Or barbecue slices of tofu about 10 minutes per side, basting frequently with marinade. Serve garnished with coriander.

*Makes 4 servings.*

# Vegetarian Lasagna

| |
|---|
| 8 oz (250 g) dried lasagna noodles |
| 10 oz (300 g) fresh spinach or 300 g package frozen chopped spinach, thawed and drained |
| 3 cups (750 mL) tomato sauce |
| 19-oz (540 mL) can tomatoes, undrained, chopped |
| 2 cups (500 mL) ricotta cheese |
| 1 egg |
| ¼ cup (50 mL) chopped fresh basil, or 1 tbsp (15 mL) dried |
| ½ tsp (2 mL) freshly ground black pepper |
| 14-oz (398 mL) can artichoke hearts, drained and coarsely chopped |
| 6 oz (175 g) soft goat cheese, crumbled |
| 1 cup (250 mL) shredded mozzarella cheese (4 oz/125 g) |
| ¼ cup (50 mL) freshly grated Parmesan cheese |

In large saucepan of boiling salted water, cook noodles about 8 minutes or until just tender. Drain.

Meanwhile, wash and trim fresh spinach. In saucepan, cook spinach just with water clinging to leaves, about 3 minutes or until wilted. Drain, squeezing out water. Chop coarsely.

In bowl, combine tomato sauce and tomatoes.

In separate bowl, combine ricotta, egg, basil and pepper.

Spread 1 cup (250 mL) tomato mixture over bottom of 13 x 9-inch (3 L) baking dish. Layer with one-third noodles, then one-third sauce. Spread half ricotta mixture on top, then half each spinach, artichoke hearts and goat cheese. Repeat layers with remaining ingredients, finishing with tomato sauce. Top with mozzarella and Parmesan.

Bake in preheated 350 F (180 C) oven about 40 minutes or until bubbling and cheese is golden.

*Makes 8 servings.*

*M*y favourite goat cheese, from Woolwich Dairies, is sold in most supermarkets. I like to use canned artichoke hearts packed in water because they're lower in fat. If you opt for the marinated ones, use two 6-oz (170 g) jars and combine half the drained marinade with the ricotta mixture. You could substitute 2 cups (500 mL) cottage cheese for the ricotta and add a thinly sliced grilled eggplant and/or a few grilled zucchini to the spinach layer.

# Meatless Moussaka

| |
|---|
| 2 medium eggplants, unpeeled |
| ¾ tsp (4 mL) salt |
| 6 potatoes, peeled |
| 1 tbsp (15 mL) lemon juice |
| 1 tbsp (15 mL) olive oil |
| 1 onion, chopped |
| 1 clove garlic, finely chopped |
| 19-oz (540 mL) can chickpeas, drained and rinsed |
| 28-oz (796 mL) can tomatoes, undrained, chopped |
| 2 tsp (10 mL) red wine vinegar |
| 2 tsp (10 mL) dried basil |
| 2 tsp (10 mL) dried oregano |
| ½ tsp (2 mL) ground cinnamon |
| ½ tsp (2 mL) salt |
| ½ tsp (2 mL) freshly ground black pepper |

## Topping:

| |
|---|
| 550 g package soft tofu, drained |
| 1 onion, quartered |
| 2 egg whites |
| 1 tbsp (15 mL) lemon juice |
| ½ cup (125 mL) freshly grated Parmesan cheese |

*A* super vegetarian version of a Greek classic, its crowning glory is the replacement for béchamel sauce — a tofu-based topping that's much lower in fat and just as tasty. Instead of roasting the eggplant slices, you could brush them lightly on both sides with olive oil and grill on a barbecue or under the broiler on medium-high heat, turning occasionally, about 15 minutes or until tender. You could grill zucchini rounds and green or red pepper strips as well and layer them with the eggplant and potato slices for a "very veggie" moussaka. If you are using home-cooked beans, you'll need 1 cup (250 mL) dried chickpeas to make about 2½ cups (625 mL) cooked.

Slice unpeeled eggplants lengthwise into pieces ¼ inch (5 mm) thick. Sprinkle each slice with salt and place in colander. Let stand 20 minutes.  Pat dry with paper towels.

Place eggplant in single layer on greased baking sheets. Bake in preheated 350 F (180 C) oven about 25 minutes or until very tender.

Cook whole potatoes in saucepan of boiling salted water about 20 minutes or until tender. Drain and cool slightly. Slice into rounds ¼ inch (5 mm) thick and sprinkle with lemon juice.

Meanwhile, heat oil in large saucepan over medium heat. Add onion and garlic.  Cook, stirring occasionally, about 4 minutes or until softened. Add chickpeas.  Cook about 3 minutes. Stir in tomatoes, vinegar, basil, oregano, cinnamon, salt and pepper. Simmer about 15 minutes or until slightly thickened.

Pour sauce into food processor work bowl.  Pulse with on/off motion just until coarsely blended.

Place eggplant slices in 13 x 9-inch (3 L) greased baking dish, overlapping slightly to cover bottom. Top with half of chickpea mixture.  Cover with potato rounds. Top with remaining chickpea mixture.

To prepare topping, in food processor, blend together tofu, onion, egg whites, lemon juice and Parmesan.  Carefully spread over chickpea mixture with back of spoon.

Bake in preheated 350 F (180 C) oven about 40 minutes or until bubbling at edges.

Place under broiler about 3 minutes or until golden-brown.

*Makes 8 servings.*

# SPICY RICE AND BEANS

| |
|---|
| *1 tbsp (15 mL) olive oil* |
| *2 cloves garlic, finely chopped* |
| *1 large onion, chopped* |
| *1 tsp (5 mL) ground cumin or curry powder* |
| *1 cup (250 mL) raw long-grain rice* |
| *2 cups (500 mL) vegetable or chicken stock* |
| *1 cup (250 mL) chunky salsa* |
| *19-oz (540 mL) can pinto, black, Romano or kidney beans, rinsed and drained* |
| *1 cup (250 mL) corn kernels* |
| *Salt and freshly ground black pepper to taste* |
| *19-oz (540 mL) can stewed tomatoes* |
| *Plain yogurt* |
| *Chopped fresh coriander* |

Heat oil in large Dutch oven over medium heat. Add garlic and onion. Cook, stirring, about 4 minutes or until soft. Stir in cumin and rice.  Cook about 1 minute. Add stock, salsa, beans, corn, salt and pepper. Stir.

Cover and cook in preheated 350 F (180 C) oven 1 to 1½ hours or until rice is tender and liquid has been absorbed.

Pour tomatoes over rice mixture, without stirring. Return to oven and cook, uncovered, 15 minutes or until heated through. Serve garnished with yogurt and coriander.

*Makes 6 servings.*

*T*his is a quick and easy family meal that I came up with for my older daughter Esther who, at the time, was a strict vegetarian. If you are using homecooked beans, you'll need 1 cup (250 mL) dried to make 2½ cups (625 mL) cooked. Use mild or hot salsa depending on your preference and vary the seasonings to taste. I like to use the Mexican or Cajun style canned tomatoes. This reheats well. I like to serve it with a green salad and crusty bread.

# TAMALE PIE

Tex-Mex food seems to fit the bill when you're in the mood for a filling, comforting meal with that palate-tingling zap of chiles. It's crowned with a yummy cornmeal topping. This is a great dish for hungry teenagers, especially penniless students who will appreciate its low price tag. For a meat version, instead of the beans, add 1 lb (500 g) ground beef to the onion mixture and cook 5 minutes or until no longer pink.

*1 tbsp (15 mL) vegetable oil*

*1 large onion, chopped*

*2 cloves garlic, finely chopped*

*Two 19-oz (540 mL) cans red kidney beans, drained and rinsed*

*2 tbsp (25 mL) chili powder*

*½ tsp (2 mL) ground cumin*

*½ tsp (2 mL) dried oregano*

*½ tsp (2 mL) salt*

*28-oz (796 mL) can tomatoes, undrained, chopped*

*1½ cups (375 mL) corn kernels*

## CORNMEAL TOPPING:

*1 cup (250 mL) all-purpose flour*

*¾ cup (175 mL) cornmeal*

*2 tbsp (25 mL) granulated sugar*

*1 tbsp (15 mL) baking powder*

*1 cup (250 mL) milk*

*1 egg*

*2 tbsp (25 mL) butter, melted*

*1½ cups (375 mL) shredded Cheddar cheese (6 oz/175 g)*

Heat oil in large skillet over medium-high heat. Add onion and garlic. Cook, stirring occasionally, about 4 minutes or until softened.

With potato masher, crush one can of beans in bowl, leaving remaining beans whole. Add beans to onion mixture, stirring to combine. Stir in chili powder, cumin, oregano and salt. Cook 1 minute. Add tomatoes and corn. Bring to a boil, reduce heat and simmer 10 minutes. Pour into 13 x 9-inch (3 L) baking dish.

To prepare topping, in bowl, combine flour, cornmeal, sugar and baking powder.

In separate bowl, whisk together milk, egg and butter. Pour into flour mixture, stirring just until moistened. Spoon topping over tamale mixture and sprinkle with cheese.

Bake in preheated 350 F (180 C) oven about 45 minutes or until topping springs back when lightly touched.

*Makes 6 servings.*

# CARAMELIZED ONION POTATO PIZZA

## CARAMELIZED ONIONS:

2 tbsp (25 mL) olive oil

1 tbsp (15 mL) butter

4 onions, coarsely chopped

Pinch salt

Pinch freshly ground black pepper

1 tbsp (15 mL) balsamic or red wine vinegar

## PIZZA:

1 large new potato, unpeeled and very thinly sliced

12 large cloves garlic, unpeeled

2 tbsp (25 mL) olive oil

1 tbsp (15 mL) chopped fresh rosemary,
or 1½ tsp/7 mL dried

¼ tsp (1 mL) salt

Pinch freshly ground black pepper

12-inch (30 cm) unbaked pizza crust

4 oz (125 g) soft goat cheese, crumbled

*P*otato pizza, which has been one of my favourites ever since I tried it in Florence, Italy, is popping up on pizza menus as a satisfying double-carbo hit. You could use herbed cream cheese or feta instead of soft goat cheese. If you can't find new potatoes, peel a regular one; Yukon Gold work really well. The caramelized onions would also be great served as an accompaniment to liver or roast chicken.
Use storebought pizza dough or try our pizza dough recipe (page 40) which makes an excellent crisp, thin crust. I like to roll the dough out on a board dusted with cornmeal; it adds crunch and helps stop the crust from sticking to the pan.

For caramelized onions, heat oil and butter in skillet over medium heat. Add onions, salt and pepper. Cook, stirring occasionally, about 15 minutes or until starting to brown. Reduce heat to low. Cook about 20 minutes more or until onions are golden and very tender. Stir in vinegar; cook 5 minutes. Taste and adjust seasoning.

Meanwhile, on rimmed baking sheet, toss potato and garlic cloves with 1 tbsp (15 mL) oil, 2 tsp (10 mL) fresh rosemary (or 1 tsp/5 mL dried), salt and pepper. Spread in single layer on baking sheet.

Bake in preheated 450 F (230 C) oven about 20 minutes or until potatoes are tender and lightly browned. Peel garlic cloves.

Spread caramelized onions over pizza crust, leaving 1-inch (2.5 cm) border. Arrange potatoes and garlic cloves in single layer over confit. Dot with goat cheese and remaining rosemary. Drizzle with remaining oil.

Bake in preheated 450 F (230 C) oven about 15 minutes or until crust and toppings are golden.

*Makes 1 pizza.*

## Pizza Dough

In small bowl, dissolve ½ tsp (2 mL) granulated sugar in 1 cup (250 mL) warm water. Sprinkle in 1 package dry active yeast (1 tbsp/15 mL) and let stand 10 minutes or until frothy.

In large bowl, combine 1⅔ cups (400 mL) all-purpose flour and 1 cup (250 mL) whole wheat flour, 2 tbsp (25 mL) olive oil and 1 tsp (5 mL) salt. Add yeast mixture, stirring until dough starts to form a ball. Turn out onto work surface, knead 7 to 10 minutes or until smooth and elastic. (Or, in food processor, blend flours, oil and salt. With machine running, gradually add yeast mixture and pulse with on/off motion until dough begins to pull away from sides of work bowl. On work surface, knead briefly to form a smooth ball.)

Place dough in large greased bowl, turning to grease all over. Cover tightly with plastic. Let rise 1 to 1½ hours or until doubled in bulk. Punch down and divide dough in half (each portion is enough for 1 pizza). If not using immediately, refrigerate or freeze in two greased plastic bags.

For each pizza, on lightly floured surface, roll out 1 portion of dough into 12-inch (30 cm) circle. Lay on greased pizza pan. Pinch dough slightly to form a raised outer rim.

In preheated 450 F (230 C) oven, bake crust 4 to 5 minutes (this makes a crisper crust). Add desired toppings and bake about 15 minutes or until crust is crisp and golden.

*Makes dough for two 12-inch (30 cm) pizzas.*

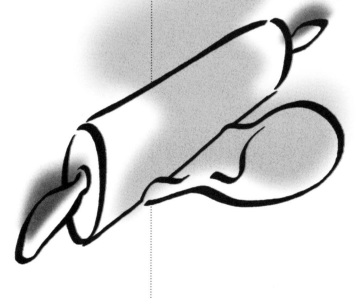

# BLACK BEAN PIZZA

*10-oz (283 g) can Pillsbury Refrigerated Pizza Crust*

*19-oz (540 mL) can black beans, drained and rinsed*

*3 tbsp (45 mL) olive oil*

*2 tbsp (25 mL) chopped fresh coriander or parsley*

*1 tsp (5 mL) ground cumin*

*1 tsp (5 mL) hot pepper sauce*

*1 clove garlic, finely chopped*

*1 cup (250 mL) shredded Monterey Jack cheese (4 oz/125 g)*

*1 cup (250 mL) shredded Cheddar cheese (4 oz/125 g)*

*¼ cup (50 mL) sliced olives*

*½ cup (125 mL) diced sweet red pepper*

*¼ cup (50 mL) chopped green onions*

*½ cup (125 mL) sour cream*

*1 cup (250 mL) chunky salsa*

Unroll dough and place in greased 12-inch (30 cm) pizza pan or 13 x 9-inch (3 L) baking dish. Starting in centre, press dough out to edges of pan.

Bake in 425 F (220 C) oven 7 to 10 minutes or until light golden.

Meanwhile, combine beans, olive oil, coriander, cumin, hot pepper sauce and garlic in bowl of food processor. Process until smooth, scraping down sides of bowl. (Or, for a coarse purée, mash bean mixture with fork or potato masher.)

Spread bean mixture over partially baked crust. Sprinkle cheeses, olives, red pepper and green onions on top.

Bake 7 to 12 minutes or until crust is deep golden-brown and cheese has melted.

Serve pizza with sour cream and salsa.

*Makes 6 to 8 servings.*

*A* nifty recipe that won first prize in the pizza crust category of the 35th Pillsbury Bake-off in 1992. Guaranteed to be a hit with kids, who could even help make it. Use homemade (page 40) or storebought pizza dough. You could use other types of beans such as red kidney, cannellini or chickpeas, but black beans have the most attractive colour. You could also substitute two 6-oz (170 g) cans chunk light tuna for the black beans.

# CORN AND BLACK BEAN TART

## CRUST:

1 cup (250 mL) all-purpose flour

½ cup (125 mL) cornmeal

1½ tsp (7 mL) chili powder

1 tsp (5 mL) ground cumin

½ tsp (2 mL) salt

½ cup (125 mL) cold butter, cubed

3 tbsp (45 mL) ice-cold water

## FILLING:

8 oz (250 g) dried black turtle beans (1 cup/250 mL), soaked overnight

1 onion, finely chopped

¼ cup (50 mL) sour cream

2 green onions, finely chopped

½ cup (125 mL) chopped fresh coriander or parsley

1 tsp (5 mL) salt

1 sweet red pepper, diced

1 cup (250 mL) shredded Cheddar cheese (4 oz/125 g)

1 jalapeño pepper, seeded and finely chopped

¼ tsp (1 mL) freshly ground black pepper

1 tbsp (15 mL) olive oil

2 cups (500 mL) corn kernels

Sour cream

To prepare crust, in food processor, combine flour, cornmeal, chili powder, cumin and salt. Add butter, pulsing with on/off motion until texture of coarse meal. Add water and process just until dough begins to clump. Turn onto work surface and knead 2 or 3 times to form a ball. Press onto bottom and sides of 11-inch (28 cm) flan pan with removable bottom. Line with parchment or waxed paper and fill with dried beans or rice as weights.

Bake in preheated 350 F (180 C) oven 10 minutes. Remove weights and paper. Bake 10 minutes longer or until edges are set and bottom looks dry.

Meanwhile, to prepare filling, drain black beans. Place in saucepan with onion and cover with water. Bring to a boil,

*This fabulous meatless main dish is another clever creation from recipe tester Heather Epp. The cornmeal crust gives a crunchy exterior while the spicy, cumin-laced black bean filling covered with melted cheese and corn kernels contributes several yummy contrasting tastes and textures. Take this elegant, colourful pie to a potluck, serve it on the patio at a summer brunch or include it in a barbecue buffet. Add a lettuce and tomato salad for a marvellous light meal.*

reduce heat and simmer about 1 hour or until tender but still whole. Drain.

In food processor, purée 1 cup (250 mL) beans, sour cream, half the green onions, half the coriander and half the salt. Spread purée over bottom of pie shell.

In bowl, combine remaining beans, green onions, coriander and salt. Add red pepper, cheese, jalapeño and black pepper.

Heat oil in skillet over medium-high heat. Add corn and cook, stirring, until slightly browned. Stir into bean mixture, tossing to combine. Pour into pie shell and smooth surface.

Bake in preheated 350 F (180 C) oven about 30 minutes or until cheese has melted. Let tart cool before serving, or it may be crumbly. Serve garnished with sour cream.

*Makes 6 servings.*

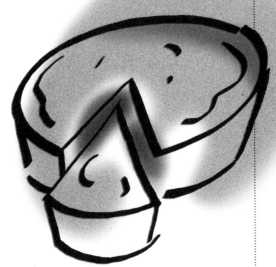

Absolutely delicious, this makes a large pie that's ideal for a party or potluck meal. Originally called Jared's Samosa Pie, the recipe comes from a cookbook called *Diane Clement at the Tomato,* in which Clement, a former athlete who owns and operates the Tomato Fresh Food Café in Vancouver, shares favourite recipes. One of her young chefs, Jared Ferguson, created this delectable dish which I have adapted slightly. The pie can easily be made ahead and reheated before serving.
Serve it with condiments like mango chutney and raita (page 47). Vary both the hot pepper flakes and the curry powder according to your taste. For an even more substantial dish, you could add cubed leftover chicken or canned tuna before baking.

# SPICY POTATO PIE

## CRUST:

| |
|---|
| 2½ cups (625 mL) all-purpose flour |
| ½ tsp (2 mL) salt |
| 1 cup (250 mL) cold butter, cubed |
| ½ cup (125 mL) ice-cold water |

## FILLING:

| |
|---|
| 4 lb (2 kg) potatoes, peeled and cubed |
| ¼ cup (50 mL) olive oil |
| 2 large onions, chopped |
| 4 cloves garlic, finely chopped |
| 2 tbsp (25 mL) finely chopped fresh ginger root |
| 4 tsp (20 mL) ground cumin |
| 4 tsp (20 mL) curry powder |
| 1 tbsp (15 mL) ground coriander |
| 2 tsp (10 mL) turmeric |
| 1 tsp (5 mL) hot pepper flakes |
| 1 tsp (5 mL) salt |
| ½ tsp (2 mL) freshly ground black pepper |
| 1 cup (250 mL) green peas |
| ¼ cup (50 mL) lemon juice |
| ¼ cup (50 mL) chopped fresh coriander or parsley |

## GLAZE:

| |
|---|
| 1 egg |
| 1 tbsp (15 mL) water |

To prepare crust, in food processor or by hand, combine flour and salt. Cut in butter until consistency of coarse meal. Add water gradually, mixing just until dough forms a ball. Turn onto work surface and knead gently a few times until smooth and soft. Wrap in plastic wrap and refrigerate 1 hour.

Meanwhile, to prepare filling, in large saucepan, cover potatoes with cold salted water. Bring to a boil, reduce heat and simmer about 10 minutes or until just tender. Drain.

Heat oil in large skillet over medium heat. Add onions, garlic and ginger. Cook, stirring, about 5 minutes or until softened. Stir in cumin, curry powder, ground coriander, turmeric, hot pepper flakes, salt and pepper. Cook about 1 minute or until fragrant. Stir in potatoes and coat well with spices. Add peas, lemon juice and fresh coriander. Cook about 1 minute.

To assemble, reserve one-third of dough for top. Roll out remaining dough into circle ⅛ inch (3 mm) thick and place in 10-inch (25 cm) springform pan, allowing dough to hang over the edge about ½ inch (1 cm).

In small bowl, whisk together egg and water. Brush crust lightly with glaze. Pour filling into crust and press evenly into pan. Roll out remaining dough to form top and overlap edges of pan. Trim and flute edges, crimping to seal.

Brush with remaining glaze and prick top crust in several places.

Bake in preheated 375 F (190 C) oven about 1¼ hours or until crust is golden.

*Makes 8 to 10 servings.*

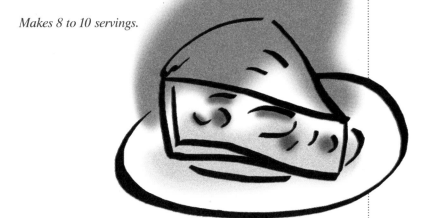

# VERSATILE VEGETABLE STEW

Use this recipe as a guide for creating your own version of a nourishing, satisfying meatless meal. You could easily substitute or add sliced or cubed eggplant, cooked pasta, potatoes, green beans, parsnips or rutabaga. You could also make a spicier version by adding a little ground cumin and/or hot pepper flakes or a dash of hot sauce. About ¼ cup (50 mL) light or 2 tbsp (25 mL) dark miso could also be added for extra flavour.

*1 tbsp (15 mL) vegetable oil*

*1 onion, chopped*

*2 stalks celery, chopped*

*1 tbsp (15 mL) chopped fresh marjoram, or 1 tsp (5 mL) dried*

*1 tbsp (15 mL) chopped fresh thyme, or 1 tsp (5 mL) dried*

*½ tsp (2 mL) salt*

*¼ tsp (1 mL) freshly ground black pepper*

*4 cups (1 L) cubed butternut squash*

*4 cups (1 L) thinly sliced cabbage*

*2 large carrots, peeled and sliced*

*28-oz (796 mL) can tomatoes, undrained, chopped*

*1½ cups (375 mL) vegetable stock*

*19-oz (540 mL) can Romano beans, kidney beans or chickpeas, drained and rinsed*

*1½cups (375 mL) corn kernels*

Heat oil in large saucepan over medium heat. Add onion. Cook about 15 minutes or until golden-brown. Stir in celery, marjoram, thyme, salt and pepper. Cook 2 minutes. Add squash, cabbage, carrots, tomatoes and stock. Cook, covered, about 20 minutes or until squash is tender. Stir in beans and corn. Cook, uncovered, 10 minutes or until vegetables are tender and sauce is slightly thickened.

*Makes 6 to 8 servings.*

# Marrakesh Vegetable Curry

| |
|---|
| 2 tbsp (25 mL) vegetable oil |
| 1 onion, chopped |
| 3 cloves garlic, finely chopped |
| 2 tbsp (25 mL) curry powder |
| 1 tbsp (15 mL) ground cumin |
| 1 tsp (5 mL) turmeric |
| 1 tsp (5 mL) salt |
| ¼ tsp (1 mL) hot pepper flakes |
| 1 large eggplant, unpeeled, cut in 1½-inch (4 cm) cubes |
| 1 lb (500 g) potatoes, peeled and cut in 1-inch (2.5 cm) cubes |
| 1 large tomato, chopped |
| 1 cup (250 mL) vegetable stock |
| 19-oz (540 mL) can chickpeas, drained and rinsed |
| 10-oz (300 g) spinach, fresh or frozen, chopped |
| ½ cup (125 mL) raisins |
| ½ cup (125 mL) slivered almonds, pine nuts or cashew pieces |
| ¼ cup (50 mL) shredded coconut (optional) |

Heat oil in large skillet over medium heat. Add onion. Cook, stirring occasionally, about 4 minutes or until softened. Add garlic, curry powder, cumin, turmeric, salt and hot pepper flakes. Cook, stirring, about 1 minute or until fragrant. Add eggplant, potatoes and tomato, stirring to coat. Pour in stock. Bring to a boil, reduce heat and simmer, covered, about 20 minutes or until vegetables are tender.

Add chickpeas, spinach and raisins. Simmer, uncovered, about 10 minutes. Garnish with nuts and coconut (if using).

*Makes 4 to 6 servings.*

## Raita

Combine 1½ cups (375 mL) plain yogurt, 1 cup (250 mL) grated cucumber, ¼ cup (50 mL) chopped fresh coriander or parsley, ½ tsp (2 mL) ground cumin and ½ tsp (2 mL) salt.

*I* adapted a recipe from Ruth Tal, owner of the popular Juice for Life health-food eateries in downtown Toronto, to come up with this very contemporary curry. Serve it over rice accompanied by condiments such as mango chutney and raita. If you are using dried beans, soak 1 cup (250 mL) dried chickpeas in plenty of cold water; let stand overnight. Drain, rinse, place in saucepan and cover with fresh water. Bring to a boil, reduce heat and simmer about 50 minutes or until tender. Use this recipe as a guideline, varying the ingredients as you like. Add or substitute veggies like green peas, green beans or cauliflower.

# KALE CHICKPEA SALAD

*A fabulous vegetarian dish that combines the nutty flavour of kale (a delicious dark, leafy green packed with iron and other nutrients) and yummy chickpeas. This makes a great side dish at a barbecue as well as a tasty light lunch or supper entrée. You could also toss the still-warm salad with hot noodles for a more substantial pasta dish.*

*1 lb (500 g) kale, stems removed, chopped (about 10 cups/2.5 L)*

*19-oz (540 mL) can chickpeas, drained and rinsed*

*2 green onions, finely chopped*

*¼ cup (50 mL) olive oil*

*3 tbsp (45 mL) lemon juice or balsamic vinegar*

*2 tsp (10 mL) chopped fresh thyme, or ¼ tsp (1 mL) dried*

*1 tsp (5 mL) Dijon mustard*

*1 clove garlic, finely chopped*

*½ tsp (2 mL) salt*

*¼ tsp (1 mL) freshly ground black pepper*

In large saucepan, steam kale about 5 minutes or until wilted. Drain and cool.

In large bowl, combine kale, chickpeas and green onions.

In small bowl, whisk together oil, lemon juice, thyme, mustard, garlic, salt and pepper.

Pour dressing over salad and toss to combine. Serve at room temperature.

*Makes 6 servings.*

# Moroccan Mixed Grain Pilaf

1 tbsp (15 mL) olive oil

1 large onion, chopped

1 tbsp (15 mL) finely chopped fresh ginger root

1 clove garlic, finely chopped

2 tsp (10 mL) curry powder

1 tsp (5 mL) ground cumin

½ tsp (2 mL) ground cinnamon

½ tsp (2 mL) turmeric

4½ cups (1.25 L) vegetable stock

1 cup (250 mL) pearl barley

½ cup (125 mL) raw long-grain brown rice

1 tsp (5 mL) salt

½ cup (125 mL) quinoa

½ cup (125 mL) millet

2 carrots, peeled and diced

19-oz (540 mL) can chickpeas, drained and rinsed

1 bunch fresh spinach or Swiss chard, thinly sliced

¼ cup (50 mL) slivered almonds or pine nuts, toasted

Grains are big these days for their nutrition (high-fibre and low-fat content in particular) and for their great taste and texture. Here I combine several grains — all sold in good bulk-food or health-food stores — and enhance them with Moroccan flavours. The addition of chickpeas (you could use other beans such as kidney or cannellini) and greens makes the dish substantial enough to be a main course. Feel free to use less of one grain and more of another as desired. You could also add a little plain yogurt and some chopped fresh herbs as a garnish at serving time.

Heat oil in large saucepan over medium heat. Stir in onion, ginger and garlic. Cook, stirring, about 4 minutes or until soft. Add curry powder, cumin, cinnamon and turmeric. Cook 1 minute. Stir in stock, barley, rice and salt. Bring to a boil, reduce heat and simmer, covered, 30 minutes.

Place quinoa in sieve and rinse well with cold water. Add to saucepan with millet and carrots. Simmer, covered, about 20 minutes or until liquid has almost been absorbed.

Place chickpeas and spinach on surface of cooking grains, without stirring. Cover and cook about 5 minutes or until spinach is just wilted and liquid has been absorbed. Turn into large serving bowl and toss with fork. Sprinkle with almonds before serving.

*Makes 6 to 8 servings.*

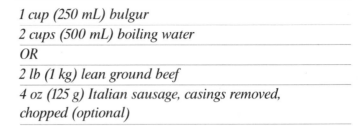

# CHILI

*Chili is one of those versatile dishes that works well with meat or without, so I've come up with two versions: one for vegetarians, the other for meat-eaters. To gild the lily and turn this into an even more filling dish, you can add a cornbread topping (Page 51).*

*This makes a lot of chili, but it does freeze very well. Vary the beans as you wish (cannellini, Romano, black beans, chickpeas or even lentils). This makes a fairly mild chili; add more jalapeños (or hot pepper flakes or hot sauce) if desired.*

*If you are using dried beans, start with 2 cups (500 mL) dried to get about 5 cups (1.25 L) cooked.*

*1 cup (250 mL) bulgur*

*2 cups (500 mL) boiling water*

*OR*

*2 lb (1 kg) lean ground beef*

*4 oz (125 g) Italian sausage, casings removed, chopped (optional)*

*1 tbsp (15 mL) olive oil*

*1 large onion, chopped*

*2 cloves garlic, finely chopped*

*2 sweet red peppers, chopped*

*1 sweet green pepper, chopped*

*2 large carrots, chopped*

*3 medium zucchini, chopped*

*3 tbsp (45 mL) chili powder*

*2 tbsp (25 mL) ground cumin*

*4 tsp (20 mL) dried oregano*

*2 jalapeño peppers, finely chopped*

*1 tsp (5 mL) salt*

*28-oz (796 mL) can tomatoes, undrained, chopped*

*5½-oz (156 mL) can tomato paste*

*3 cups (750 mL) vegetable or beef stock*

*2 tbsp (25 mL) brown sugar*

*Two 19-oz (540 mL) cans red kidney beans, drained and rinsed*

*1 cup (250 mL) corn kernels*

For vegetarian version, soak bulgur in hot water while preparing remaining ingredients.

For meat version, in large saucepan or Dutch oven over medium-high heat, brown ground beef and sausage about 7 minutes or until no longer pink. Remove from pan.

Heat oil in Dutch oven over medium heat. Add onion and cook, stirring occasionally, about 4 minutes or until softened. Stir in garlic, red and green peppers, carrots and zucchini. Cook 5 minutes. Add chili powder, cumin, oregano, jalapeños and salt. Cook 1 minute, stirring to coat vegetables. Stir in tomatoes, tomato paste, stock and sugar. Bring to a boil, reduce heat and simmer 10 minutes.

Add bulgur or beef mixture and beans. Simmer 20 minutes or until slightly thickened. Stir in corn. Cook 5 minutes.

*Makes 12 servings (beef) or 10 servings (vegetarian).*

## Cornbread Topping

This cornbread topping is enough to cover about 8 cups (2 L) of chili in a 13 x 9-inch (3 L) casserole. You could omit the jalapeños in the topping and/or mix in a few chopped green onions.

In large bowl, combine 1 cup (250 mL) cornmeal, 1 cup (250 mL) all-purpose flour, 2 tbsp (25 mL) granulated sugar, 2 tsp (10 mL) baking powder and 1 tsp (5 mL) salt.

In separate bowl, whisk together 1 cup (250 mL) milk, 2 beaten eggs, 2 tbsp (25 mL) melted butter and 2 finely chopped jalapeños. Pour into dry mixture, stirring just until combined.

Pour 6 to 8 cups (1.5 to 2 L) chili into 13 x 9-inch (3 L) baking dish. Spread cornmeal mixture over top.

Bake in preheated 350 F (180 C) oven 30 minutes or until cornmeal is golden and springs back when lightly touched.

*Makes 8 servings.*

# RIBOLLITA

From Massimo Capra, chef at Prego della Piazza in downtown Toronto, comes this slow-cooked Italian country staple. A great meatless dish to serve to a crowd with a salad, bread and white wine. You could add some chopped cooked bacon or pancetta if you don't mind meat, as well as any number of other vegetables. Capra likes to rub the bread with garlic and brush it lightly with olive oil before toasting.

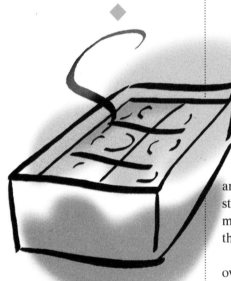

*1 cup (250 mL) dried pea (navy) beans*

*2 tbsp (25 mL) olive oil*

*4 cloves garlic, finely chopped*

*4 bay leaves*

*1 large onion, finely chopped*

*2 large carrots, peeled and diced*

*1 stalk celery, diced*

*8 cups (2 L) vegetable stock or water*

*3 cups (750 mL) shredded cabbage*

*2 large tomatoes, chopped*

*2 tsp (10 mL) chopped fresh thyme, or ½ tsp (2 mL) dried*

*½ tsp (2 mL) salt*

*¼ tsp (1 mL) freshly ground black pepper*

*½ loaf Italian bread, cut in slices ½ inch (1 cm) thick (about 16 slices)*

*⅔ cup (150 mL) freshly grated Parmesan cheese*

Cover beans with cold water and soak overnight. (Or do a quick soak by bringing beans to a boil; turn off heat and let stand 1 hour.) Drain.

Heat oil in large saucepan over medium heat. Add garlic and bay leaves. Cook about 3 minutes. Stir in onion, carrots and celery. Cook about 4 minutes or until softened. Pour in stock and bring to a boil. Reduce heat and simmer about 40 minutes or until beans are tender. Stir in cabbage, tomatoes, thyme, salt and pepper. Simmer 5 minutes. Remove bay leaves.

Meanwhile, toast bread slices in preheated 350 F (180 C) oven about 15 minutes or until lightly browned.

In 13 x 9-inch (3 L) baking dish, pour one-third of bean mixture. Top with half the bread slices. Repeat layers, ending with bean mixture and making sure all bread is moistened. Sprinkle with Parmesan.

Bake in preheated 350 F (180 C) oven 45 minutes or until top is golden and ribollita is bubbling.

*Makes 8 servings.*

# Seafood and Poultry

# SEAFOOD STEW

This is one of my favourite dinner-party dishes. It's easy to make (albeit a tad pricey, depending on the seafood you use), low in fat and absolutely delicious. I make the seasoned broth a day ahead (it could even be made earlier and frozen), then heat it up and drop the prepared seafood in at the last minute for its very brief cooking time.

2 tbsp (25 mL) olive oil

1 onion, chopped

2 cloves garlic, finely chopped

19-oz (540 mL) can tomatoes, chopped, or 2 cups (500 mL) chopped fresh tomatoes

1½ cups (375 mL) dry white wine

2 cups (500 mL) fish stock

1 tbsp (15 mL) chopped fresh thyme, or ½ tsp (2 mL) dried

1 tbsp (15 mL) chopped fresh oregano, or ½ tsp (2 mL) dried

1 tbsp (15 mL) chopped fresh basil, or ½ tsp (2 mL) dried

½ tsp (2 mL) hot pepper flakes

Pinch saffron (optional)

Salt and freshly ground black pepper to taste

8 oz (250 g) fresh cod, haddock, bluefish or grouper, skinned, boned and cut in chunks

8 oz (250 g) fresh salmon, skinned, boned and cut in chunks

8 oz (250 g) fresh monkfish, skinned, boned and cut in chunks

8 oz (250 g) fresh scallops, cleaned and halved

8 oz (250 g) large shrimp, peeled and deveined (about 12)

## GARNISH:

Homemade croutons

Sour cream or plain yogurt

Fresh dill or coriander sprigs

Heat oil in large saucepan over medium heat. Add onion and garlic. Cook, stirring, about 5 minutes or until softened. Add tomatoes, wine, fish stock, thyme, oregano, basil, hot pepper flakes and saffron (if using). Bring to a boil, reduce heat and simmer about 20 minutes or until slightly thickened. Add salt and pepper. (Stew may be made ahead to this point, covered and refrigerated up to 1 day.)

Add cod, salmon and monkfish. Cook 3 minutes. Add scallops and shrimp. Cook 2 to 4 minutes or until fish flakes when tested with a fork, scallops are opaque and shrimp are pink. Taste and adjust seasoning.

Ladle stew into large soup bowls. Top with croutons, sour cream and a sprig of dill.

*Makes 6 servings.*

## Homemade Croutons

In large bowl, toss 6 cups (1.5 L) bread cubes with ¼ cup (50 mL) olive oil and 4 finely chopped cloves garlic. Spread on baking sheet and bake in preheated 350 F (180 C) oven, stirring occasionally, about 20 minutes or until golden and crisp.

## Homemade Fish Stock

In large saucepan, barely cover 1½ lb (750 g) bones and heads (gills removed) of lean white fish with cold water. Bring just to a boil over medium-high heat. Reduce heat to a simmer; skim any froth from surface.

Add ½ cup (125 mL) dry white wine, 1 small onion, 1 stalk celery, 1 clove garlic, and a pinch of thyme. Simmer 20 minutes. Strain, discarding bones and vegetables. Freeze leftover stock.

# DAVE'S FISH BATTER

2 cups (500 mL) all-purpose flour

1¼ tsp (6 mL) baking powder

1 tsp (5 mL) salt

1 egg

1½ cups (375 mL) water

½ cup (125 mL) beer

Vegetable oil for deep-frying

2 lb (1 kg) fish fillets, such as cod, halibut, sole, perch

In large bowl, whisk together flour, baking powder, salt, egg, water and beer until smooth. Let stand 20 minutes.

In deep-fryer or wok, heat oil to 375 F (190 C).

Cut fish fillets into serving-sized portions if necessary; pat dry. Dip fish into batter, turning to coat evenly. Fry, 3 at a time, about 5 minutes or until crisp and golden-brown on all sides, turning frequently. Remove with slotted spoon to plate lined with paper towels. Let stand 1 minute before serving.

*Makes 6 servings.*

*This amazing recipe came from Dave Johnston, owner of the family-owned North Toronto landmark, Penrose Fish and Chips. He shared it with* Toronto Star *readers for a Father's Day feature. Bound to be a hit when you feel like an old-fashioned, nutritionally incorrect meal of fish and chips! Depending on how thickly you coat the fish, there may be enough batter for more than 2 lb (1 kg).*

# MICK JAGGER'S SHRIMP CURRY

1 tbsp (15 mL) vegetable oil

1 large onion, finely chopped

2 tsp (10 mL) curry powder

400 mL can coconut milk

2 tbsp (25 mL) lime or lemon juice

½ tsp (2 mL) garam masala

1½ lb (750 g) shrimp, peeled and deveined

Salt and cayenne pepper to taste

¼ cup (50 mL) chopped fresh coriander or parsley

Heat oil in large skillet over medium heat. Add onion and cook, stirring, about 5 minutes or until softened. Stir in curry powder. Cook 30 seconds. Add coconut milk, lime juice and garam masala. Bring to a boil. Stir in shrimp, reduce heat and simmer 4 to 5 minutes or until shrimp are bright pink and just cooked through. Stir in salt, cayenne and coriander.

*Makes 6 servings.*

*We found this dish in an out-of-print book of rock stars' favourite recipes. If Mick really did invent it – and who am I to doubt him – he cooks as well as he sings! Serve over steamed rice with stir-fried veggies and/or a salad. Garam masala is a spice blend sold in some supermarkets and most East Indian food shops.*

# Impossible Tuna, Spinach and Cheese Pie

*300 g package frozen chopped spinach,
thawed and drained*

*Two 6½-oz (184 g) cans chunk light tuna, drained*

*1½ cups (375 mL) shredded Swiss cheese (6 oz/175 g)*

*1 onion, chopped*

*1¼ cups (300 mL) biscuit baking mix*

*1¾ cups (425 mL) milk*

*4 eggs*

*½ tsp (2 mL) salt*

*Pinch freshly ground black pepper*

In greased 13 x 9-inch (3 L) baking dish, combine spinach, tuna, cheese and onion.

In bowl or blender, whisk or blend together biscuit mix, milk, eggs, salt and pepper. Pour over tuna mixture.

Bake in preheated 350 F (180 C) oven about 30 minutes or until knife inserted in centre comes out clean.

*Makes 6 to 8 servings.*

*We* adapted a back-of-the-box Bisquick recipe to come up with this first-rate, easy dish. "Impossible" because it magically makes its own crust, this is great served with a big salad and crusty bread. Use a round quiche or flan pan for an attractive presentation and substitute cooked chicken or turkey for the tuna and/or other veggies such as blanched broccoli, snow peas or asparagus for the spinach.

# GRILLED SALMON
# WITH THREE SAUCES

*2 lb (1 kg) salmon fillets or steaks, or 1 whole side*

*¼ cup (50 mL) lemon juice*

*2 tsp (10 mL) chopped fresh thyme, or ¼ tsp (1 mL) dried*

*1 tsp (5 mL) Dijon mustard*

*¼ tsp (1 mL) salt*

Using tweezers, remove any small bones from salmon. Place on baking sheet.

In small bowl, whisk together lemon juice, thyme, mustard and salt. Brush over salmon and refrigerate at least 1 hour or up to 4 hours.

On greased grill over medium heat, grill salmon (skin side down, if using fillets or whole side) about 10 minutes per inch (2.5 cm) of thickness, or until fish flakes easily when tested with fork.

Serve hot or cold with sauce passed separately.

*Makes 6 servings.*

# FAKE HOLLANDAISE SAUCE:

*1 cup (250 mL) plain yogurt*

*3 egg yolks*

*1 tsp (5 mL) cornstarch*

*1 tbsp (15 mL) lemon juice*

*1 tsp (5 mL) Dijon mustard*

*¼ tsp (1 mL) salt*

*¼ tsp (1 mL) granulated sugar*

*2 tbsp (25 mL) chopped fresh chives or green onions*

*1 tbsp (15 mL) chopped fresh thyme, or ¼ tsp (1 mL) dried*

In double boiler over barely simmering water, whisk together yogurt, egg yolks and cornstarch. Cook, stirring, about 7 minutes or until slightly thickened. Remove from heat. Whisk in lemon juice, mustard, salt and sugar. Stir in chives and thyme.

*Makes about 1¼ cups (300 mL).*

## Yogurt Dill Sauce:

*1 cup (250 mL) plain yogurt*

*¼ cup (50 mL) chopped fresh dill*

*1 tsp (5 mL) Dijon mustard*

*¼ tsp (1 mL) horseradish (optional)*

*Salt and freshly ground black pepper to taste*

In small bowl, stir together yogurt, dill, mustard and horseradish (if using). Season with salt and pepper.

*Makes about 1¼ cups (300 mL).*

## Sauce Gribiche:

*1 cup (250 mL) mayonnaise*

*2 hard-boiled eggs, finely chopped*

*½ cup (125 mL) chopped red onion*

*¼ cup (50 mL) chopped dill pickle*

*2 tbsp (25 mL) capers, chopped*

*1 tbsp (15 mL) chopped fresh tarragon,
or ½ tsp (2 mL) dried*

*2 tsp (10 mL) lemon juice*

*¼ tsp (1 mL) salt*

*¼ tsp (1 mL) freshly ground black pepper*

In small bowl, combine mayonnaise, eggs, onion, pickle, capers, tarragon, lemon juice, salt and pepper. Refrigerate until ready to serve.

*Makes about 1½ cups (375 mL).*

# Perfect Paella

When my recipe tester Heather Epp went on a trip to Spain, I gave her the following mandate: bring back a recipe for the ultimate paella. On her return, she produced this – a delectable version adapted for Canadian ingredients. The dish makes a beautiful presentation and is great for a party because the preparation can be done in advance with minimal last-minute attention. Many things can be added or substituted as the mood strikes – squid, lobster and rabbit are all delicious, traditional additions. Substitute short-grain Italian rice if you can't find Spanish rice. If you are using large clams, steam them about 4 minutes before adding them to the paella. If you are making your own chicken stock, add the shrimp shells to it for extra flavour.

1 sweet red pepper

¼ cup (50 mL) olive oil

8 oz (250 g) boneless, skinless chicken breast, cut in 1-inch (2.5 cm) pieces

8 oz (250 g) medium shrimp, peeled and deveined

1 large onion, chopped

2 cloves garlic, finely chopped

2 large tomatoes, chopped

4 oz (125 g) chorizo sausage or smoked ham, chopped

½ tsp (2 mL) hot pepper flakes

1½ cups (375 mL) raw short-grain Spanish rice

½ cup (125 mL) dry white wine

3 cups (750 mL) chicken stock

¼ tsp (1 mL) saffron threads

½ tsp (2 mL) salt

¼ tsp (1 mL) freshly ground black pepper

8 oz (250 g) halibut, cod or other firm white fish fillet, skinned and cut in 1-inch (2.5 cm) pieces

6 mussels

6 small clams

½ cup (125 mL) green peas

Place whole pepper in preheated 450 F (230 C) oven 15 to 20 minutes or until charred. Place in bowl. Cover and let stand until cool.

Meanwhile, heat 2 tbsp (25 mL) oil in 10-inch (25 cm) paella pan or large skillet with sloping sides, over medium-high heat. Add chicken. Cook about 4 minutes or until lightly browned. Remove to plate.

Add shrimp to skillet. Cook about 3 minutes, or until just pink, and transfer to plate with chicken.

Reduce heat to medium. Stir in onion and garlic and cook about 4 minutes or until golden. Add tomatoes, chorizo and hot pepper flakes. Cook, stirring occasionally, about 6 minutes or until liquid from tomatoes has evaporated.

Stir in rice. Cook 1 minute. Add wine, stirring to combine well. Pour in chicken stock, saffron, salt and pepper. Bring to a boil, reduce heat and simmer 15 minutes.

Meanwhile, peel charred skin from red pepper. Remove core and seeds and cut pepper into thin strips.

Stir chicken, shrimp and halibut into rice mixture. Nestle mussels and clams in rice with opening edges facing up. Sprinkle red pepper strips and peas between shells.

Place in preheated 400 F (200 C) oven 15 minutes or until rice is tender and liquid has almost been absorbed. Cover and let stand 10 minutes before serving.

*Makes 4 to 6 servings.*

# CHICKEN COUSCOUS SALAD

| |
|---|
| *3 lb (1.5 kg) chicken, roasted* |
| *2 tbsp (25 mL) lemon juice or wine vinegar* |
| *¼ cup (50 mL) olive oil* |
| *¼ tsp (1 mL) curry powder* |
| *Dash hot pepper sauce* |
| *Salt and freshly ground black pepper to taste* |
| *1½ cups (375 mL) chicken stock* |
| *1 cup (250 mL) couscous* |
| *3 green onions, chopped* |
| *½ cup (125 mL) cooked chickpeas* |
| *1 sweet red pepper, chopped* |
| *⅓ cup (75 mL) raisins* |
| *⅓ cup (75 mL) toasted pine nuts or slivered almonds* |
| *¼ cup (50 mL) chopped fresh coriander or parsley* |

Remove meat from chicken. Cut into bite-sized pieces.

In small bowl, whisk together lemon juice, olive oil, curry powder, hot pepper sauce, salt and pepper.

Bring chicken stock to boil in medium saucepan. Add couscous and stir. Cover and remove from heat. Let stand 5 minutes. Transfer to large serving bowl.

Toss couscous with chicken, green onions, chickpeas, red pepper, raisins and dressing. Mix well, fluffing with fork. Serve at room temperature, garnished with pine nuts and fresh coriander.

*Makes 4 to 6 servings.*

*A* delicious, quick dinner-party, buffet or potluck dish, this is really easy if you make it with one of those rotisserie chickens from the supermarket or local Portuguese churrasqueira. For a meatless version, use vegetable stock, omit the chicken and add the whole 19-oz (540 mL) can of chickpeas. All the couscous I've bought in Metro (both packaged and from bulk-food stores) is precooked and only needs hot liquid to be reconstituted.

*Cindy Pawlcyn,
owner/chef of
the Mustard Grill, one of
Napa Valley's most
established restaurants,
makes this using quail,
but chicken is just as good.
I got the recipe on a visit to
California, where this dish
was served at a reception
for food writers. You can grill
the chicken as described
here or roast it in the oven.
The combo of spicy
marinade and sweetish/sour
plum sauce (the latter can
easily be made ahead)
is simply superb.
Anise seed star is sold in
some supermarket spice
sections and most specialty
spice or bulk-food stores.*

# Mongolian Chicken with Plum Sauce

*3 lb (1.5 kg) chicken, cut in serving pieces*

## Marinade:

*¾ cup (175 mL) hoisin sauce*

*2 tbsp (25 mL) rice vinegar*

*1 tbsp (15 mL) soy sauce*

*1½ tsp (7 mL) granulated sugar*

*1 tsp (5 mL) finely chopped fresh ginger root*

*1 tsp (5 mL) dark sesame oil*

*1 tbsp (15 mL) chopped fresh coriander or parsley*

*1 green onion, finely chopped*

*½ tsp (2 mL) freshly ground black pepper*

*½ small jalapeño pepper, seeded and chopped*

*Dash hot pepper sauce*

## Plum Sauce:

*1¼ cups (300 mL) water*

*2 tbsp (25 mL) dry white wine*

*1 tbsp (15 mL) Port or Madeira*

*¼ cup (50 mL) brown sugar*

*½-inch (1 cm) piece fresh ginger root, thinly sliced*

*2 cloves garlic, finely chopped*

*1 tsp (5 mL) whole black peppercorns*

*Juice and finely grated rind of ½ orange*

*Juice and finely grated rind of ½ lemon*

*1 whole dried anise seed star (optional)*

*3 large purple plums, pitted and chopped*

*Salt and freshly ground black pepper to taste*

Place chicken in single layer in shallow non-metallic dish.

To prepare marinade, in bowl, stir together hoisin, vinegar, soy sauce, granulated sugar, chopped ginger, sesame oil, coriander, green onion, pepper, jalapeño and hot pepper sauce. Pour over chicken and turn to coat well. Cover and marinate in fridge at least 4 hours but preferably overnight.

To prepare sauce, in saucepan, combine water, wine, Port, brown sugar, sliced ginger, garlic, peppercorns, orange and lemon juice along with rind and anise seed star. Bring to a boil, reduce heat and simmer 30 minutes. Add plums and simmer 30 minutes.

Strain mixture through coarse sieve, pushing as much plum flesh through as possible. (Do not use blender because of whole spices.) Add salt and pepper.

Remove chicken from marinade; discard marinade. Grill chicken 30 minutes on lightly greased grill over medium heat, turning frequently to prevent burning, about 30 minutes or until no longer pink inside.

Serve chicken drizzled with or dunked in warm plum sauce. (Leftover sauce keeps, refrigerated, about 1 week.)

*Makes 6 servings.*

## CHICKEN LIVERS AU VINAIGRE

*1 lb (500 g) chicken livers, trimmed of sinew*

*2 tbsp (25 mL) vegetable oil*

*1 small onion, chopped*

*3 cloves garlic, finely chopped*

*2 tbsp (25 mL) red wine vinegar*

*2 tbsp (25 mL) balsamic vinegar*

*½ cup (125 mL) chicken stock or water*

*1 large tomato, seeded and chopped*

*1 tsp (5 mL) chopped fresh sage, or ¼ tsp (1 mL) dried*

*Salt and freshly ground black pepper to taste*

*Dash hot pepper sauce*

*2 tbsp (25 mL) chopped fresh parsley or green onions*

Heat 2 tsp (10 mL) oil in large, heavy-bottomed skillet over high heat. Cook livers in batches, turning when browned. Keep in single layer for even cooking. Transfer to bowl.

Reduce heat to medium. Stir in remaining oil and onion. Cook, stirring, 4 minutes. Add garlic and cook about 1 minute, without browning. Pour in vinegars and cook about 5 minutes or until reduced by half. Add stock, tomato, sage and juices from livers. Bring to a boil, reduce heat and simmer 2 to 3 minutes. Stir in salt, pepper, hot pepper sauce and cooked livers. Heat gently but do not boil. Serve sprinkled with parsley.

*Makes 4 servings.*

*T*his dish was inspired by one I saw talented chef and knowledgeable foodie Jacques Pépin prepare at a demo many years ago. I like liver on the rare side, but if you prefer it well done, cook it a minute or two longer. A superb nutritious, quick and inexpensive meal that's great served with boiled potatoes, rice or pasta and a salad. I sometimes make this for myself as a weeknight meal and just eat it with salad and some crunchy French or Italian bread to sop up the delectable sauce.

# POTLUCK POULET

*Two 3-lb (1.5 kg) chickens, cut in pieces*

*1 cup (250 mL) pitted prunes, quartered*

*1 cup (250 mL) pitted green olives, sliced*

*½ cup (125 mL) dried tomatoes, sliced*

*¼ cup (50 mL) chopped fresh marjoram or oregano, or 4 tsp (20 mL) dried*

*2 tbsp (25 mL) capers*

*6 cloves garlic, finely chopped*

*¼ cup (50 mL) olive oil*

*2 tbsp (25 mL) balsamic vinegar*

*2 tbsp (25 mL) red wine vinegar*

*1 tsp (5 mL) salt*

*½ tsp (2 mL) freshly ground black pepper*

*½ cup (125 mL) brown sugar*

*1 cup (250 mL) dry white wine*

*¼ cup (50 mL) chopped fresh parsley*

Place chicken pieces in single layer in one or two large baking dishes.

In bowl, combine prunes, olives, dried tomatoes, marjoram, capers, garlic, oil, vinegars, salt and pepper. Pour over chicken. Cover and refrigerate overnight. Remove chicken from marinade.

In large skillet, brown chicken pieces in batches. Return to marinade. Sprinkle chicken with brown sugar. Pour wine around edges of dish.

Bake, uncovered, in preheated 350 F (180 C) oven, basting frequently, about 45 minutes or until juices run clear and meat is no longer pink inside. Transfer chicken to platter and sprinkle with parsley. Skim fat from sauce. Pour sauce around chicken or pass separately.

*Makes 8 to 10 servings.*

*A* fabulous dish that, in various incarnations, has been doing the rounds of dinner parties since it first appeared in *The Silver Palate Cookbook* almost two decades ago. You could easily double it for a really large crowd and increase or reduce the prunes, olives, dried tomatoes and capers according to taste. You could also omit the step of browning the chicken before baking; this will make the recipe quicker and easier, but browning does add flavour and colour to this delectable concoction. You could also remove the chicken skin before marinating to reduce fat. The perfect dish to put out at a buffet meal, this tastes even better if it's made a day ahead.

# JERK CHICKEN

2 tbsp (25 mL) garlic powder

1 tbsp (15 mL) granulated sugar

1 tbsp (15 mL) ground allspice

1 tbsp (15 mL) dried thyme

1½ tsp (7 mL) hot pepper flakes, or to taste

1½ tsp (7 mL) freshly ground black pepper

1½ tsp (7 mL) dried sage

1 tsp salt

¾ tsp (4 mL) grated nutmeg

¾ tsp (4 mL) ground cinnamon

½ cup (125 mL) white, cider or wine vinegar

½ cup (125 mL) orange juice

¼ cup (50 mL) olive oil

¼ cup (50 mL) soy sauce

Juice of 1 lime or lemon

1 onion, chopped

3 green onions, chopped

1 Scotch bonnet pepper, seeded and finely chopped

6 single chicken breasts

In large, shallow baking dish, combine garlic powder, sugar, allspice, thyme, hot pepper flakes, pepper, sage, salt, nutmeg and cinnamon. Stir in vinegar, orange juice, oil, soy sauce, lime juice, onion, green onions and Scotch bonnet, mixing until smooth. Place chicken breasts in marinade and refrigerate at least 4 hours or up to 24 hours.

Remove chicken from marinade and reserve marinade. Broil or grill chicken 20 to 25 minutes, turning occasionally and basting with marinade at intervals, until no longer pink inside.

Pour remaining marinade into small saucepan. Bring to a boil and simmer 5 minutes. Pour sauce over chicken or serve on side.

*Makes 6 servings.*

*A* fabulous version of a Caribbean standard that's an improvement on the traditional one, in my opinion, because it comes with its own lusciously spicy sauce. You could use chicken parts instead of breasts and easily double the recipe for a crowd. Scotch bonnet peppers (sold in Caribbean stores and some supermarkets) are very hot; substitute a jalapeño or some hot sauce or hot pepper flakes if desired. You can remove the skin from the chicken to reduce fat, if you wish. In warm weather, this is excellent done on the barbecue, but it can also be baked in the oven with terrific results. In season, you could use fresh instead of dried herbs; just increase the amounts. You could also use finely chopped fresh garlic instead of garlic powder.

# CHICKEN CACCIATORE

This was inspired by a recipe from chef Paul Prudhomme of New Orleans, one of this continent's best cooks. A wonderful version of an old standby, it has a delectably rich sauce and is great served with pasta, mashed potatoes or risotto. It tastes even better if it's made a day or so ahead.

*1 tbsp (15 mL) salt*

*1 tbsp (15 mL) dried basil*

*2 tsp (10 mL) dried oregano*

*2 tsp (10 mL) dried thyme*

*2 tsp (10 mL) garlic powder*

*1 tsp (5 mL) freshly ground black pepper*

*¼ tsp (1 mL) cayenne pepper*

*4 lb (2 kg) chicken pieces*

*2 tbsp (25 mL) olive oil*

*1 large onion, chopped*

*2 large sweet green peppers, chopped*

*12 oz (375 g) mushrooms, sliced (4 cups/1 L)*

*6 cloves garlic, finely chopped*

*1 cup (250 mL) dry red wine*

*2 cups (500 mL) chicken stock*

*28-oz (796 mL) can tomatoes, undrained, chopped*

*5½-oz (156 mL) can tomato paste*

*2 tbsp (25 mL) brown sugar*

In small bowl, combine salt, basil, oregano, thyme, garlic powder, pepper and cayenne. Rub half of spice mixture into chicken pieces, coating well.

Heat oil in large, heavy-bottomed saucepan over medium-high heat. Brown chicken, in batches, until golden on all sides. Remove chicken to plate and reduce heat to medium.

Add onion to saucepan. Cook, stirring, about 4 minutes or until softened and slightly browned. Add green peppers, mushrooms and garlic. Cook about 7 minutes or until mushrooms are tender and liquid has almost evaporated. Stir in remaining spice mixture. Pour in wine, stock, tomatoes, tomato paste and sugar. Bring to a boil, reduce heat and add chicken pieces. Simmer, uncovered, about 25 minutes or until chicken is no longer pink inside.

*Makes 6 servings.*

# CREAMY LEMON CHICKEN

8 single boneless, skinless chicken breasts

¼ cup (50 mL) lemon juice

2 tsp (10 mL) finely grated lemon rind

¼ cup (50 mL) chopped fresh herbs
(e.g., basil, thyme, oregano, tarragon, chives
or a combination), or 1 tbsp (15 mL) dried

½ cup (125 mL) dry white wine

1 tsp (5 mL) liquid honey

¼ tsp (1 mL) salt

¼ tsp (1 mL) freshly ground black pepper

1 tbsp (15 mL) olive oil

½ cup (125 mL) chicken stock

½ cup (125 mL) whipping cream

Trim excess fat from chicken breasts. Place in non-metallic baking dish.

In bowl, whisk together lemon juice and rind, herbs, wine and honey. Pour over chicken. Cover and refrigerate 2 hours, turning once. Remove chicken, draining well. Reserve marinade. Sprinkle chicken with salt and pepper.

Heat oil in large skillet over medium-high heat. Cook chicken breasts in batches, about 10 minutes, turning occasionally to brown both sides. Remove to platter.

Add marinade to skillet, stirring to scrape up brown bits from bottom. Bring to a boil, reduce heat slightly and simmer about 3 minutes or until reduced by half. Stir in stock and cream and bring to a boil.

Return chicken breasts to skillet. Cook over low heat 3 to 4 minutes or until chicken is no longer pink inside.

*Makes 8 servings.*

*I* love this recipe because it's quick, easy, fairly low in cost, calls for few ingredients and tastes delicious. It is simple enough to be a weekday family meal but is also great for entertaining. What's more, the small amount of whipping cream adds smooth richness to the sauce without a lot of fat, since each serving contains only a spoonful of cream. Serve garnished with lots of fresh parsley or watercress and lemon slices. For an elegant presentation, you could strain the sauce before serving to remove the flecks of herbs.
Use fresh lemon juice if you can (the bottled juice is very strong), and although this is best made with fresh herbs, you could substitute dried. Try the herbs suggested here (a combination works best) and decide which flavours you prefer.

## CHICKEN STUFFED UNDER SKIN

*3 to 4-lb (1.5 to 2 kg) roasting chicken*

*2 tsp (10 mL) olive oil*

Using fingers, gently ease skin away from flesh over breasts. Place stuffing between flesh and skin. Tie legs together and tuck wings behind back. Place chicken breast side up on greased rack in roasting pan. Rub chicken with oil.

Roast in preheated 325 F (160 C) oven about 25 minutes per pound until juices run clear or until meat thermometer inserted in thigh reads 185 F (85 C).

Remove chicken from pan and discard string. Let stand 10 minutes. Serve with pan juices, if desired.

*Makes 4 to 6 servings.*

## BASIL-STUFFED CHICKEN

*½ cup (125 mL) fresh basil leaves*

*4 cloves garlic, finely chopped*

*3 tbsp (45 mL) butter, at room temperature*

*Salt and freshly ground black pepper to taste*

*1 lemon, halved*

Reserve 6 basil leaves. Finely chop remaining basil.

In bowl, combine chopped basil, garlic and butter. Refrigerate, covered, 15 minutes or until just firm.

Spread mixture between skin and breast meat of chicken. Press skin back over.

Sprinkle cavity of chicken with salt and pepper. Place lemon halves in cavity. Place remaining whole basil leaves in bottom of roasting pan to flavour juices. Truss chicken and roast as above.

*E*ver since a Hungarian cook at a restaurant where I was once working showed me how to roast chicken stuffed under the skin with a mixture of giblets, herbs and breadcrumbs, there's been no turning back.
I now stuff chicken under the skin with everything from whole garlic cloves to spoonfuls of herbed goat cheese. Here are three variations on this yummy theme.

# Rosemary Feta-stuffed Chicken

*3 oz (90 g) feta or soft goat cheese, crumbled*
*(½ cup/125 mL)*

*2 tbsp (25 mL) chopped fresh oregano,*
*or ½ tsp (2 mL) dried*

*1 tbsp (15 mL) chopped fresh rosemary,*
*or ½ tsp (2 mL) dried*

*½ tsp (2 mL) salt (omit if using feta)*

*¼ tsp (1 mL) freshly ground black pepper*

In small bowl, combine feta, oregano, rosemary, salt
(if using) and pepper.

Spread mixture evenly between skin and breast meat. Truss
chicken and cook as above.

# Fruit-stuffed Chicken

*1 tsp (5 mL) olive oil*

*1 small onion, finely chopped*

*1 clove garlic, finely chopped*

*1 tsp (5 mL) curry powder (optional)*

*¼ tsp (2 mL) salt*

*Pinch freshly ground black pepper*

*¼ cup (50 mL) chopped prunes*

*¼ cup (50 mL) chopped dried apricots*

*¼ cup (50 mL) raisins*

Heat oil in small skillet over medium heat. Add onion.
Cook, stirring, about 3 minutes or until softened. Stir in garlic,
curry powder, salt and pepper. Cook about 1 minute or until
fragrant. Stir in prunes, apricots and raisins.

Stuff fruit mixture evenly between skin and breast meat.
Truss chicken and cook as above.

# TANDOORI CHICKEN

*I have been making this fabulous version of an East Indian classic for many years. Traditionally, the dish is cooked in a tandoor (brick) oven, and a bright-red food dye is added to the marinade, but I prefer not to use it. A perfect dinner-party entrée, potluck offering or picnic item. I sometimes use a whole chicken instead of pieces. This is great hot or cold. Serve it with steamed basmati rice laced with saffron or turmeric and topped with raisins and toasted almonds, chutney, raita (page 99) and the Indian flatbread naan (page 113).*

*3 to 4-lb (1.5 to 2 kg) chicken pieces*

*2 tsp (10 mL) coriander seeds*

*1 tsp (5 mL) cumin seeds*

*1 cup (250 mL) plain yogurt*

*2 cloves garlic, finely chopped*

*1 tbsp (15 mL) finely chopped fresh ginger root*

*1 tsp (5 mL) salt*

*Juice of 1 lemon*

*½ tsp (2 mL) hot pepper flakes, or to taste*

*½ tsp (2 mL) turmeric*

*Lettuce leaves*

*Lime and tomato wedges*

*Sprigs of fresh coriander or parsley*

Prick holes in chicken skin. Place in large shallow dish in single layer.

Toast coriander seeds and cumin seeds in dry, heavy skillet over low heat, shaking constantly, 2 to 3 minutes or until fragrant. Grind in blender or coffee mill until powdery.

In bowl, stir together ground spices, yogurt, garlic, ginger, salt, lemon juice, hot pepper flakes and turmeric. Pour over chicken. Cover and refrigerate overnight.

Place chicken in single layer in large baking dish or roasting pan, making sure pieces are well coated with marinade.

Cook in preheated 350 F (180 C) oven about 1 hour or until crisp and brown. Serve on a bed of lettuce and garnish with lime and tomato wedges and fresh coriander.

*Makes 4 to 6 servings.*

# BISTRO CHICKEN

9 fresh tomatoes (about 3 lb/1.5 kg)

3 tbsp (45 mL) olive oil

4 lb (2 kg) chicken, cut in serving pieces

4 onions, cut in wedges

6 cloves garlic, finely chopped

1¼ cups (300 mL) dry white wine

⅓ cup (75 mL) tomato paste

1 tbsp (15 mL) brown sugar

4 tsp (20 mL) chopped fresh tarragon,
or 1 tsp (5 mL) dried

1 tbsp (15 mL) chopped fresh thyme,
or ¾ tsp (4 mL) dried

½ tsp (2 mL) salt

¼ tsp (1 mL) freshly ground black pepper

¼ tsp (1 mL) hot pepper sauce

3 stalks celery, chopped

*Local field tomatoes, bursting with juice and flavour, are combined with fresh herbs in this yummy, easy-to-make dish from Foodland Ontario. It can easily be made ahead as a great dinner-party dish. Out of season, substitute an undrained 28-oz (796 mL) can of plum tomatoes. Fresh basil or other favourite herbs could be substituted for those used here.*

Core tomatoes and cut shallow X on bottoms. Place in large saucepan of boiling water about 30 seconds. Remove with slotted spoon and plunge into bowl of cold water immediately. Peel off skins and chop tomatoes.

Heat oil in wide, deep saucepan or Dutch oven over medium-high heat. Add chicken pieces, in batches if necessary, cooking about 5 minutes per side until deep golden-brown.

Reduce heat to medium. Add onions, cooking about 4 minutes or until softened. Stir in garlic. Cook 1 minute. Add 1 cup (250 mL) wine, stirring to scrape brown bits from bottom of pan. Simmer until wine is reduced by half. Stir in tomatoes, tomato paste, brown sugar, tarragon, thyme, salt, pepper and hot pepper sauce.

Add chicken, spooning sauce over top. Bring just to a boil, reduce heat and simmer, covered, 35 minutes. Stir in celery and cook 10 minutes or until celery is still crisp and chicken is no longer pink inside. Stir in remaining wine.

*Makes 4 to 6 servings.*

# BROWN RICE TURKEY PILAF

1 tbsp (15 mL) vegetable oil

1 large onion, chopped

3 cloves garlic, finely chopped

1 tbsp (15 mL) finely chopped fresh ginger root

1 tbsp (15 mL) chopped fresh thyme,
or ½ tsp (2 mL) dried

½ tsp (2 mL) ground cumin

¼ tsp (1 mL) hot pepper flakes

3 cups (750 mL) chicken stock

4 cups (1 L) diced cooked turkey

1 cup (250 mL) raw long-grain brown rice

½ cup (125 mL) dried tomatoes, sliced (1½ oz/45 g)

1 tsp (5 mL) salt

½ tsp (2 mL) freshly ground black pepper

¼ cup (50 mL) chopped fresh parsley

Heat oil in large Dutch oven. Add onion, garlic, ginger, thyme, cumin and hot pepper flakes. Reduce heat to medium. Cook, stirring, about 5 minutes or until onion has softened. Pour in chicken stock and bring to a boil. Stir in turkey, rice, tomatoes, salt and pepper.

Cover and bake in preheated 350 F (180 C) oven about 1 hour or until liquid has been absorbed. Sprinkle with parsley before serving.

*Makes 6 servings.*

*T*his superb dish was inspired by a recipe I once saw demonstrated by ace chef/foodie Jacques Pépin when he was on one of his visits to Toronto. I streamlined it to come up with what has become my favourite way to use up leftover turkey or almost any meat, for that matter.
If you are using oil-packed dried tomatoes, drain them before using to reduce the fat. This is great served with a sauced side dish such as ratatouille (page 92).

# TURKEY TORTILLA CASSEROLE

2 tbsp (25 mL) butter or olive oil

⅓ cup (75 mL) cornmeal

19-oz (540 mL) can Mexican-style stewed tomatoes

3 cups (750 mL) chicken stock

1 tbsp (15 mL) olive oil

1 sweet red pepper, chopped

1 medium zucchini, chopped

1 jalapeño pepper, finely chopped (optional)

1 tbsp (15 mL) chili powder

½ tsp (2 mL) salt

½ tsp (2 mL) freshly ground black pepper

4 cups (1 L) diced cooked turkey

2 cups (500 mL) corn kernels

½ cup (125 mL) sliced olives

8 oz (250 g) tortilla chips

Melt butter in medium saucepan over medium heat. Stir in cornmeal and cook 1 minute, stirring constantly. Add tomatoes and stock. Bring to a boil, reduce heat and simmer about 20 minutes, or until slightly thickened.

Heat oil in skillet over medium heat. Stir in red pepper, zucchini and jalapeño (if using). Cook about 5 minutes or until vegetables are softened and lightly browned. Add chili powder, salt and pepper. Cook about 1 minute or until vegetables are coated.

In 13 x 9-inch (3 L) baking dish, combine vegetable mixture, tomato sauce, turkey, corn and olives. Stand tortilla chips up in close rows in casserole so that points are up.

Bake in preheated 350 F (180 C) oven about 40 minutes or until bubbling and thick.

*Makes 6 servings.*

*An* excellent way to use up that leftover turkey from the holidays, this Tex-Mex dish is also great made with leftover chicken. Garnish each serving with a dollop of sour cream or plain yogurt and some chopped fresh coriander and you've got a meal elegant enough to serve guests.

# TURKEY ENCHILADAS

*Another wonderful way to use up leftover turkey or chicken, this recipe could easily be doubled. You could also substitute Cheddar for the Monterey Jack cheese. Garnish, if you wish, with sour cream and chopped fresh coriander.*

*1 tbsp (15 mL) olive oil*

*2 onions, chopped*

*2 cloves garlic, finely chopped*

*1 sweet red or green pepper, chopped*

*2 tbsp (25 mL) chili powder*

*1 tsp (5 mL) ground cumin*

*1 tsp (5 mL) dried oregano*

*19-oz (540 mL) can tomatoes, drained (juices reserved), chopped*

*1 cup (250 mL) salsa*

*2 cups (500 mL) diced cooked turkey*

*½ cup (125 mL) chopped fresh coriander or parsley*

*2 cups (500 mL) shredded Monterey Jack cheese (8 oz/250 g)*

*Eight 10-inch (25 cm) flour tortillas*

Heat oil in large skillet over medium heat. Add onions, garlic and sweet pepper. Cook, stirring, about 5 minutes, or until softened. Stir in chili powder, cumin and oregano. Cook 1 minute. Add tomatoes, salsa, turkey and coriander. Cook just until mixture comes to a boil. Stir in 1 cup (250 mL) cheese.

Divide turkey mixture among tortillas, spreading filling along centre. Roll up and place seam side down in 13 x 9-inch (3 L) baking dish. Pour reserved tomato juice over and top with remaining cheese.

Bake in preheated 350 F (180 C) oven about 40 minutes or until cheese has melted and sauce is bubbling at edges.

*Makes 4 servings.*

# Meat

# CABBAGE ROLLS WITH TOMATO SAUCE

*You could use just 1¼ lb (625 g) ground beef and omit the ground pork if desired for this yummy old-fashioned version of a homey favourite.*

| |
|---|
| *1 large cabbage, core removed* |
| *1 lb (500 g) ground beef* |
| *4 oz (125 g) ground pork* |
| *½ cup (125 mL) raw rice* |
| *1 onion, finely chopped* |
| *2 tsp (10 mL) salt* |
| *½ tsp (2 mL) freshly ground black pepper* |
| *3 cups (750 mL) tomato sauce* |
| *¼ cup (50 mL) white vinegar* |
| *¼ cup (50 mL) packed brown sugar* |

Bring very large saucepan of water to boil. Plunge whole head of cabbage into water and boil 5 minutes. Lift out of water, place on plate and cool slightly. Remove outer leaves. If inner leaves are hard to remove, return to boiling water 2 to 3 minutes. You will need about 12 leaves. With sharp knife, shave off part of thick stem, thinning it to make rolling easier.

In bowl, combine beef, pork, rice, onion, salt, pepper and 1 cup (250 mL) tomato sauce, mixing well. Place about ¼ cup (50 mL) meat mixture at stem end of a cabbage leaf. Roll up envelope style. Place in large, heavy-bottomed skillet. Repeat with remaining leaves and filling.

In small bowl, combine remaining tomato sauce, vinegar and sugar. Pour over rolls. Cover and place over medium heat. Bring to a boil, reduce heat and simmer 1½ hours or until cabbage is very tender and filling is no longer pink inside.

*Makes about 12 cabbage rolls.*

## Lazy Cabbage Roll Casserole

Using same ingredients as above, try this quick version. Chop cabbage and boil 5 minutes. Drain.

In large skillet, cook ground meat and onion about 5 minutes or until browned (or add a 19-oz/540 mL can of beans to browned onions for a meatless version). Stir in 1 cup (250 mL) rice, cabbage, tomato sauce, vinegar, sugar, salt and pepper. Bring to a boil. Pour into 13 x 9-inch (3 L) baking dish. Add 2 cups (500 mL) water.

Cover and bake in preheated 375 F (190 C) oven 1½ to 2 hours or until cabbage is very tender. Add a little water during cooking if necessary.

# TEX-MEX LASAGNA

1 tbsp (15 mL) vegetable oil

1 large onion, chopped

2 cloves garlic, finely chopped

1½ lb (750 g) ground beef

2 tbsp (25 mL) chili powder

1½ tsp (7 mL) ground cumin

1 tsp (5 mL) dried oregano

½ tsp (2 mL) cayenne pepper

½ tsp (2 mL) salt

¼ tsp (1 mL) hot pepper flakes (optional)

14-oz (398 mL) can stewed tomatoes

2 cups (500 mL) ricotta cheese

1 cup (250 mL) shredded Monterey Jack cheese
(4 oz/125 g)

1 egg, lightly beaten

Twelve 6-inch (15 cm) corn tortillas

1 cup (250 mL) shredded lettuce

1 large tomato, chopped

4 green onions, chopped

½ cup (125 mL) sliced black olives

½ cup (125 mL) shredded Cheddar cheese (2 oz/60 g)

No food snob, I am a big fan of hearty Tex-Mex fare that's well prepared. Using the layered lasagna theme as a guide, we came up with this delicious dish. It can be made ahead, either cooked or uncooked, to serve at a party, potluck or buffet meal. It is also great reheated – if there are any leftovers. Vary the heat as desired by using more or fewer hot pepper flakes. For a meatless version, use two 19-oz (540 mL) cans red kidney beans, drained, rinsed and liquid reserved, instead of the ground beef. Stir into onion mixture along with ½ cup (125 mL) of their reserved liquid.

Heat oil in large skillet over medium-high heat. Add onion and garlic. Cook 3 minutes or until softened. Stir in ground beef. Cook 5 minutes or until no longer pink. Pour off fat. Stir in chili powder, cumin, oregano, cayenne, salt and hot pepper flakes (if using). Cook 1 minute. Stir in tomatoes. Bring to a boil, reduce heat and simmer 5 minutes.

In bowl, combine ricotta, Monterey Jack and egg.

Line bottom and sides of greased 13 x 9-inch (3 L) baking dish with half the tortillas. Spread beef or bean mixture over bottom. Top with remaining tortillas. Cover evenly with cheese mixture.

Bake in preheated 350 F (180 C) oven about 35 minutes or until top is just set. Remove from oven and cover with diagonal rows of shredded lettuce, tomato, green onions, olives and Cheddar.

*Makes 8 servings.*

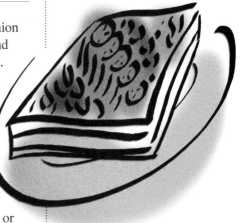

## CRUNCHY GOAT CHEESE BURGERS

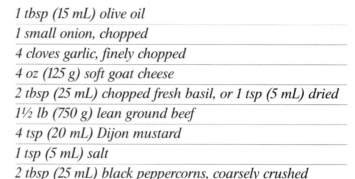

What a delectable twist this is on a tried-and-true theme – the surprise mouthful of goat cheese inside the burger and the crunch of spicy peppercorns on the outside.
To coarsely crush peppercorns, enclose them in a large sheet of waxed paper, folded in half and crimped at the edges to form an envelope. Pound with a mallet or crush with the bottom of a heavy skillet. Very thinly sliced Parmesan cheese and fresh basil leaves are a great addition to the usual condiments for these burgers.
You could use blue cheese in place of goat's. These are great barbecued or broiled.

| |
|---|
| 1 tbsp (15 mL) olive oil |
| 1 small onion, chopped |
| 4 cloves garlic, finely chopped |
| 4 oz (125 g) soft goat cheese |
| 2 tbsp (25 mL) chopped fresh basil, or 1 tsp (5 mL) dried |
| 1½ lb (750 g) lean ground beef |
| 4 tsp (20 mL) Dijon mustard |
| 1 tsp (5 mL) salt |
| 2 tbsp (25 mL) black peppercorns, coarsely crushed |

Heat oil in small skillet over medium heat. Add onion and garlic; cook, stirring, 5 minutes or until soft but not browned.

In small bowl, combine goat cheese and basil until smooth. Shape into six small patties.

In separate bowl, combine ground beef, onion mixture, mustard and salt. Shape into 12 patties. Top half the meat patties with a goat cheese patty; cover with remaining beef patties, pinching edges to seal. Lightly coat each burger with peppercorns. Grill over medium heat, turning once, 10 to 15 minutes.

*Makes 6 burgers.*

## MARINATED FLANK STEAK

This is a popular quick meal at my house, where we sometimes eat the steak along with your usual two veg or, as a change, sliced thinly either hot or at room temperature on top of salad. I love the flavour and even the slightly chewy texture of flank steak, a relatively inexpensive cut now sold in most supermarkets. The marinated steak can also be broiled or cooked over high heat in a non-stick pan, or it can be thinly sliced and stir-fried.

| |
|---|
| 2 tbsp (25 mL) barbecue sauce |
| 2 tbsp (25 mL) red wine vinegar |
| 1 tbsp (15 mL) olive oil |
| 1 tsp (5 mL) Dijon mustard |
| 1 clove garlic, finely chopped |
| ¼ tsp (1 mL) freshly ground black pepper |
| 1 lb (500 g) flank steak |

In shallow baking dish large enough to hold steak flat, combine barbecue sauce, vinegar, oil, mustard, garlic and pepper. Place steak in sauce, turning to coat. Cover and refrigerate at least 2 hours or overnight, turning occasionally.

On greased grill over medium heat, grill steak 5 to 7 minutes for medium–rare, turning once. Let stand, covered, 5 minutes before slicing thinly across the grain.

*Makes 4 servings.*

# OLD-FASHIONED MEATLOAF

*1 lb (500 g) lean ground beef*

*8 oz (250 g) ground veal*

*8 oz (250 g) ground pork*

*1 tsp (5 mL) Worcestershire sauce*

*2 eggs, lightly beaten*

*1½ cups (375 mL) cracker crumbs*
*(about 44 soda crackers) or breadcrumbs*

*42-g package dry onion soup mix*

*¾ cup (175 mL) ketchup*

*½ cup (125 mL) water*

*4 strips bacon (optional)*

*1½ cups (375 mL) tomato sauce*

In large bowl, combine ground beef, veal and pork. Add Worcestershire, eggs, cracker crumbs, soup mix, ketchup and water. Combine well.

Form meat mixture into loaf shape and place in 11 x 7-inch (2 L) baking dish. Crisscross bacon strips (if using) on top of loaf. Pour tomato sauce over top and down sides of meatloaf.

Bake in 350 F (180 C) oven 1½ hours or until meat thermometer registers 160 F (70 C). Let stand 20 minutes before slicing. Skim excess fat from sauce if necessary. Pour sauce over sliced meatloaf or serve on the side.

*Makes 6 to 8 servings.*

You could use all ground beef or just ground chicken or turkey in this superb, tried-and-true rendition of a family favourite. We found that dry onion soup packages vary in size, although most are in this ballpark – you'll need about ¼ cup (125 mL). Add a dash of hot sauce if you like a little zing in your meatloaf. This is great served with mashed potatoes and a green veg. Leftovers make the best sandwiches.

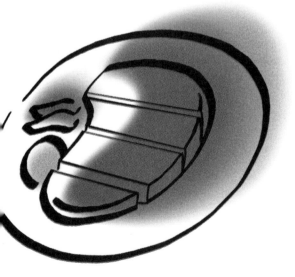

# Beef Beer Stew

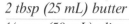

*O*ne word of caution when making this amazing stew inspired by the classic French version called Carbonnade. Do not use light beer. Only the full-fledged stuff – preferably a dark or amber ale – gives the right depth of flavour. I find that cooking this (and any braised meat) in the oven gives it a really rich taste.

Delicious with boiled potatoes, pasta or rice and a tossed salad, this is one of those dishes that will win raves all round. It tastes even better a day after it's made and can easily be frozen.

*2 tbsp (25 mL) butter*

*¼ cup (50 mL) olive oil*

*6 onions, cut in thin wedges*

*2½ lb (1.25 kg) stewing beef, cut in 1-inch (2.5 cm) cubes*

*¼ cup (50 mL) all-purpose flour*

*12-oz (341 mL) bottle beer*

*28-oz (796 mL) can tomatoes, undrained, chopped*

*¼ tsp (1 mL) dried oregano*

*¼ tsp (1 mL) dried thyme*

*¼ tsp (1 mL) salt*

*¼ tsp (1 mL) freshly ground black pepper*

*6 oz (175 g) mushrooms, thickly sliced (2 cups/500 mL)*

*Chopped fresh parsley*

Heat 1 tbsp (15 mL) butter and 1 tbsp (15 mL) oil in large, ovenproof saucepan or Dutch oven over medium heat. Add onion. Cook, stirring occasionally, about 20 minutes or until beginning to colour. Reduce heat to low and cook about 10 minutes or until very tender and golden. Transfer onions to bowl and wipe saucepan.

Lightly coat meat cubes with flour; shake off excess.

Heat 1 tbsp (15 mL) butter and 1 tbsp (15 mL) oil in saucepan over medium-high heat. Cook meat in batches (pieces should not touch), browning well on all sides. Remove to bowl with onions. Drain off any fat.

Add beer to saucepan. Bring to a boil, stirring to scrape up brown bits from bottom. Boil about 3 minutes or until reduced by one-third. Stir in onions and beef along with tomatoes, oregano, thyme, salt and pepper. Bring just barely to a boil.

Cover and cook in preheated 325 F (160 C) oven or over low heat on top of stove about 2 hours or until meat is fork-tender.

Heat remaining 2 tbsp (25 mL) olive oil in large skillet over medium-high heat. Add mushrooms. Cook, stirring occasionally, about 5 minutes or until browned. Stir into stew. Serve garnished with parsley.

*Makes 6 servings.*

# JOHN'S BRISKET

*1 tbsp (15 mL) vegetable oil*

*4 to 5-lb  (2 to 2.5 kg) beef brisket, trimmed of excess fat*

*2 lb (1 kg) carrots or sweet potatoes,*
*peeled and cut in chunks*

*5 cups (1.25 L) tomato juice or vegetable cocktail*

*2 tbsp (25 mL) pickling spice*

*Salt and freshly ground black pepper to taste*

Heat oil in roasting pan or large Dutch oven over medium-high heat. Sear meat on all sides until deep brown. Remove from heat. Turn brisket so it is fat side down in roasting pan.  Add carrots to pan.

In large bowl, combine tomato juice and pickling spice. Pour over meat.

Cook, covered, in preheated 325 F (160 C) oven about 4 hours or until meat is very tender. Transfer brisket to platter.

In batches, purée meat juices and carrots in food processor until smooth. Season with salt and pepper.

Cut meat into ½-inch (1 cm) slices.  Pour some puréed sauce over meat. Serve remaining sauce on side. To make ahead, purée sauce as above. Do not slice meat; chill separately from sauce. (The meat is much easier to slice when cooled.) Slice meat and arrange in large shallow baking dish. Spoon enough sauce over meat to cover completely. Cover pan and reheat in preheated 350 F (180 C) oven about 40 minutes or until heated through and bubbly. Heat remaining sauce and pass separately.

*Makes 8 to 10 servings.*

*A* homey dish from my colleague and friend John Kessler, food editor of the *Denver Post*. You could make it as part of a traditional Jewish meal or for no reason at all. Great served with egg noodles.

# POT ROAST

| |
|---|
| *3-lb (1.5 kg) boneless chuck, rump, blade or short-rib roast* |
| *½ tsp (2 mL) salt* |
| *Pinch freshly ground black pepper* |
| *1 tbsp (15 mL) vegetable oil* |
| *2 large onions, chopped* |
| *4 stalks celery, sliced* |
| *4 large carrots, peeled and sliced* |
| *2 cups (500 mL) beef stock* |
| *1 cup (250 mL) dry red wine* |
| *2 tbsp (25 mL) brown sugar* |
| *1 tbsp (15 mL) tomato paste* |
| *1 tsp (5 mL) dried basil* |
| *½ tsp (2 mL) dried thyme* |
| *2 tsp (10 mL) balsamic vinegar* |
| *1 tsp (5 mL) cornstarch dissolved in 1 tbsp (15 mL) water* |

*E*very household needs a good pot roast recipe for those wintry days when nothing else quite hits the spot. The beauty of this dish is that it not only improves a day or two after it's made, but leftovers are great to take to work as is or made into hot or cold sandwiches. You could use a 19-oz (540 mL) can of tomatoes in this instead of tomato paste and reduce the stock to 1 cup (250 mL). (When you are using only a small amount of tomato paste, you can freeze the remainder in ice cube trays.) This recipe makes a lot of sauce, probably the best part of the dish anyway. Serve with mashed potatoes and your favourite canned or frozen veg!

Rub beef with salt and pepper.

Heat oil in heavy-bottomed Dutch oven over medium-high heat and brown roast on all sides. Reduce heat to medium. Add onions, celery and carrots. Cook, stirring occasionally, 3 minutes. Add stock, wine, brown sugar, tomato paste, basil and thyme. Bring just to a boil, reduce heat and simmer, covered, 3 hours or until meat is very tender. Transfer roast to serving platter.

To make gravy, purée cooking liquid and vegetables in food processor or blender. Pour 2 cups (500 mL) purée into small saucepan (freeze remaining purée to use in soup, gravy or as pasta sauce base) and bring to a boil. Stir in vinegar.

Whisk in cornstarch mixture. Boil, stirring, 2 to 3 minutes or until sauce has thickened slightly.

*Makes 6 servings.*

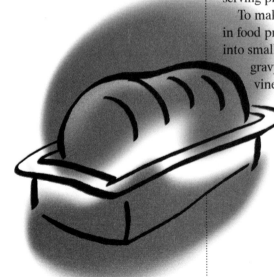

# SOUTHERN BARBECUED PORK

*3-lb (1.5 kg) boneless pork butt or pork shoulder roast*

*1 tsp (5 mL) vegetable oil*

*1 cup (250 mL) tomato sauce*

*¼ cup (50 mL) cider vinegar*

*¼ cup (50 mL) Worcestershire sauce*

*¼ cup (50 mL) packed brown sugar*

*½ tsp (2 mL) celery seed*

*½ tsp (2 mL) chili powder*

*¼ tsp (1 mL) salt*

*¼ tsp (1 mL) freshly ground black pepper*

*Dash hot pepper sauce*

Pierce surface of roast with sharp knife in several places.

Heat oil in Dutch oven or ovenproof casserole over medium-high heat. Add roast and brown on all sides. Drain off fat.

In small bowl, combine tomato sauce, vinegar, Worcestershire sauce, brown sugar, celery seed, chili powder, salt, pepper and hot sauce. Pour over roast and bring just to a boil.

Cook, covered, in preheated 325 F (160 C) oven, basting occasionally, about 2 hours or until fork-tender. Let stand 10 minutes before serving.

*Makes 6 servings.*

*A* fantastic recipe with roots in the Southern United States, this rib-hugging roast is perfect for a winter's day served with mashed potatoes or baked sweet potatoes and collard greens. Yet more proof that some of the best dishes are the most simple. You could use bottled or homemade tomato sauce; the old-fashioned canned stuff is really good in this dish.

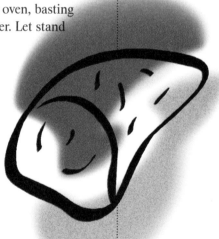

# RABBIT RAGOUT

*2 to 3-lb (1 to 1.5 kg) rabbit, cut in 12 pieces,
washed and patted dry*

## MARINADE:

*1½ cups (375 mL) dry red wine*

*6 cloves garlic, crushed*

*2 bay leaves*

*½ tsp (2 mL) freshly ground black pepper*

## RAGOUT:

*4 tbsp (50 mL) olive oil*

*1 onion, chopped*

*1 clove garlic, finely chopped*

*4 oz (125 g) prosciutto, pancetta or bacon, cut in strips*

*2 tbsp (25 mL) all-purpose flour*

*2 tsp (10 mL) brown sugar*

*5 cups (1.25 L) beef or chicken stock*

*¼ cup (50 mL) tomato paste*

*2 tbsp (25 mL) chopped fresh rosemary,
or 1 tsp (5 mL) dried*

*2 tbsp (25 mL) chopped fresh thyme, or 1 tsp (5 mL) dried*

*½ tsp (2 mL) salt*

*Pinch freshly ground black pepper*

*¾ cup (175 mL) pitted black olives*

*½ cup (125 mL) raisins (optional)*

*2 tbsp (25 mL) chopped fresh parsley*

*Finely grated rind of 1 orange*

Place rabbit in large, shallow, non-metallic dish. For marinade, in bowl, combine wine, crushed garlic, bay leaves and pepper. Pour over rabbit. Cover and refrigerate 24 hours, turning occasionally. Remove rabbit from marinade and pat dry. Discard marinade.

In large ovenproof casserole, heat 2 tbsp (25 mL) oil over medium heat. Add onion and chopped garlic. Cook 3 minutes. Add prosciutto and cook 5 minutes. Transfer to dish.

Heat remaining 2 tbsp (25 mL) oil in casserole over medium-high heat. Brown rabbit on all sides, in batches if necessary. Sprinkle with flour and brown sugar. Toss gently

*R*abbit is a low-fat, flavourful meat that is quite often found in supermarkets these days and makes a pleasant change from chicken. Serve this yummy stew over pasta, risotto, mashed potatoes or your favourite grain.

and cook about 3 minutes. Add reserved onion mixture, stock, tomato paste, rosemary, thyme, salt and pepper. Cook, covered, in preheated 350 F (180 C) oven 45 minutes. Remove rabbit to plate; cool slightly. Pull meat from bones and cut into chunks or shred into small pieces. Discard bones. Return meat to sauce. Before serving, stir in olives, raisins (if using), parsley and orange rind. Simmer gently about 5 minutes.

*Makes 6 servings.*

# RISOTTO WITH
# SAUSAGE AND MUSHROOMS

| |
|---|
| ½ oz (15 g) dried porcini mushrooms |
| ½ cup (125 mL) boiling water |
| 2 tbsp (25 mL) olive oil |
| 2 sweet Italian sausages, casings removed, finely chopped |
| 1 large onion, finely chopped |
| 2 cups (500 mL) raw Arborio rice |
| 1 cup (250 mL) dry white wine |
| 5 cups (1.25 L) chicken stock, hot |
| 1 cup (250 mL) green peas |
| ½ cup (125 mL) freshly grated Parmesan cheese |
| 2 green onions, chopped |
| Salt and freshly ground black pepper to taste |

In small bowl, combine mushrooms and boiling water. Let stand 15 minutes or until softened. Strain through a coffee filter or cheesecloth, reserving liquid. Coarsely chop mushrooms.

Meanwhile, heat oil in large saucepan over medium heat. Add sausage and cook, stirring, about 5 minutes or until no longer pink. Add onion and mushrooms. Cook about 4 minutes or until softened. Stir in rice. Cook 1 minute. Add wine, stirring until completely absorbed. Add 1 cup (250 mL) hot stock and reserved mushroom liquid. Continue stirring until almost absorbed. Add 1 cup (250 mL) more stock and continue stirring and adding liquid in this manner about 25 minutes or until all stock has been incorporated and rice is tender and very creamy. Stir in peas, Parmesan, green onions, salt and pepper. Cook 2 minutes.

*Makes 6 to 8 servings.*

You could easily substitute other cooked meat for the sausage and other greens for the peas in this dish, but do use Arborio rice – the special short-grain Italian rice used in risottos. I shared this dish when Food section colleagues contributed recipes to an article about how to cook great food at budget prices. It's popular with children and is also great to serve at a dinner party as a main course or, without the sausage, as a side dish. Vary the ingredients to suit your mood, the occasion or the contents of your fridge.

# BRAISED LAMB SHANKS

This is one of my favourite braised dishes, perfect for supper on a cold winter's day. Lamb shanks are versatile, flavourful and inexpensive. Serve them over garlic mashed potatoes (page 97), pasta or rice and you've got a great weekday family meal that can be made (even frozen) and then heated at the last minute. Garnish them with fresh herbs and you've got a fine dish to serve with a full-bodied red wine at a dinner party. The frozen shanks from New Zealand are available year-round at supermarkets and are reasonably priced.

*6 lamb shanks*

*½ tsp (2 mL) salt*

*¼ tsp (1 mL) freshly ground black pepper*

*2 tbsp (25 mL) olive oil*

*1 large onion, chopped*

*2 large carrots, peeled and sliced*

*2 stalks celery, chopped*

*12 cloves garlic (about one head), peeled*

*1 cup (250 mL) dry red wine*

*2 cups (500 mL) beef or chicken stock*

*19-oz (540 mL) can tomatoes, undrained,
or 3 large fresh tomatoes, chopped*

*½ tsp (2 mL) dried thyme*

*1 tsp (5 mL) dried rosemary*

*2 tbsp (25 mL) balsamic vinegar*

Trim lamb shanks of fat. Sprinkle with salt and pepper.

Heat 1 tbsp (15 mL) oil in large skillet over medium-high heat. In batches, brown lamb on all sides. Remove to large casserole dish or small roasting pan.

Reduce heat under skillet to medium and heat remaining oil. Add onion, carrots, celery and garlic to skillet. Cook, stirring, about 7 minutes or until softened. Pour in wine, stirring to scrape up brown bits from bottom of pan. Add stock, tomatoes, thyme and rosemary. Bring to a boil and remove from heat. Pour mixture over lamb.

Cover and cook in preheated 350 F (180 C) oven 2 hours or until very tender. Stir vinegar into sauce.

*Makes 6 servings.*

# Vegetables and Side Dishes

# THREE GREENS

*This delicious dish can also be made with rapini, Swiss chard, beet greens, bok choy, spinach or watercress but, as they are more delicate than the greens used here, reduce the total cooking time to about 15 minutes. Inspired by the Deep South but fashionable these days almost everywhere, this would be great as a sidekick to any roast meat or fish, or with meatless fare such as pasta with beans. Healthy, hearty and good for the soul.*

*1 tbsp (15 mL) olive oil*

*1 onion, diced*

*2 cloves garlic, finely chopped*

*2 tbsp (25 mL) cider vinegar*

*2 cups (500 mL) vegetable, chicken or beef stock*

*1 tsp (5 mL) granulated sugar*

*1 bunch collard greens (1 lb/500 g), washed and sliced*

*1 bunch kale (1 lb/500 g), washed and sliced*

*1 bunch dandelion greens (1 lb/500 g), washed and sliced*

*Salt and freshly ground black pepper to taste*

*About 12 cherry tomatoes, halved*

Heat oil in large saucepan over medium heat. Add onion and cook, stirring, about 3 minutes or until softened. Stir in garlic and cook 1 minute. Add vinegar, stock, sugar and collards. Bring to a boil, reduce heat and cook, covered, about 15 minutes. Add kale and cook 15 minutes longer. Add dandelion greens and cook 20 minutes more. Stir in salt, pepper and tomatoes before serving.

*Makes 8 servings.*

# ASIAN CABBAGE

3 tbsp (45 mL) rice vinegar or cider vinegar

2 tbsp (25 mL) soy sauce

1 tbsp (15 mL) cornstarch

1 tbsp (15 mL) granulated sugar

1 tsp (5 mL) hot Oriental chili paste

4 tsp (20 mL) dark sesame oil

2 tbsp (25 mL) finely chopped fresh ginger root

2 cloves garlic, finely chopped

4 oz (125 g) mushrooms, sliced (1½ cups/375 mL)

1 large head Napa cabbage, thinly sliced (12 cups/3 L)

¼ cup (50 mL) chicken stock or water

Salt and freshly ground black pepper to taste

¼ cup (50 mL) chopped fresh coriander or parsley

In small bowl, combine vinegar, soy sauce, cornstarch, sugar and chili paste.

Heat sesame oil in wok or large skillet over high heat. Stir in ginger, garlic and mushrooms. Cook, stirring, about 1 minute. Add cabbage and chicken stock. Cook, stirring to coat cabbage, about 3 minutes or until just wilted.

Make a well in centre of wok. Pour in vinegar mixture, stirring constantly until clear and thickened. Toss with cabbage. Season with salt and pepper. Garnish with coriander.

*Makes 4 to 6 servings.*

*I* am a big fan of cabbage. It's inexpensive, tasty, low-cal, loaded with fibre and very versatile. Often I simply stir-fry shredded cabbage with a little vegetable oil in a wok along with chopped ginger and garlic, then add chicken stock and soy sauce to finish. This more exotic concoction highlights cabbage's many virtues, and it is wonderful served with braised meat. For a vegetarian main dish, you could add a 19-oz (540 mL) can of chickpeas or other beans along with the vinegar mixture.

Napa cabbage is the light-coloured, oval-shaped Oriental cabbage sold in any Chinatown and many supermarkets. You could substitute bok choy, red cabbage or regular cabbage if desired. Substitute any vegetables you like for the mushrooms, as well; diced red pepper or slivered carrots would be great.

# FAKE FETTUCCINE ZUCCHINI

*2 sweet red peppers*

*5 medium zucchini (2 lb/1 kg), unpeeled*

*2 tbsp (25 mL) vegetable oil*

*2 tbsp (25 mL) dry sherry*

*1 tsp (5 mL) rice vinegar or cider vinegar*

*Salt and freshly ground black pepper to taste*

With potato peeler or other vegetable cutter, cut peppers and zucchini into thin fettuccine-shaped strips.

Heat oil in wok or large skillet over medium-high heat. Stir in red pepper strips. Cook about 1 minute. Add zucchini and cook, stirring gently, 2 minutes.

Pour in sherry and vinegar. Cover and cook 2 to 3 minutes or until just wilted but still crisp. Add salt and pepper.

*Makes 4 servings.*

## Spaghetti Squash

Prick squash in several places and bake whole in preheated 350 F (180 C) oven for about 45 minutes or until soft when pricked with fork. Slice squash in half horizontally. Scoop out the pasta-like strands and toss with sautéed onions, garlic and fresh tomatoes (or your favourite pasta sauce) for a low-cal, delectable main or side dish.

*I* got this idea for "noodles" made out of zucchini strips when I was in New York one year for the James Beard Awards, and a group of American women chefs cooked a wondrous buffet meal. It comes from Barbara Tropp, owner/chef of the China Moon Cafe in San Francisco. Tropp likes to use both green and yellow zucchini; do not peel them.
This could be a side dish for almost any meal (especially good at a mid-summer barbecue when those abundant zucchini are at their peak), but it would also be great as a main dish served like pasta topped with a favourite tomato or meat sauce and sprinkled with freshly grated Parmesan. You could also toss the hot zucchini with crumbled goat cheese and chopped fresh tomatoes. Spaghetti squash is a veg that naturally mimics pasta when it is cooked and the "spaghetti" strands are scooped out.

# Eugenia's Funghi al Forno

⅓ cup (75 mL) chopped fresh parsley

6 cloves garlic, finely chopped

1 tsp (5 mL) hot pepper flakes

1½ lb (750 g) assorted fresh mushrooms
(e.g., shiitake, oyster, brown)

½ cup (125 mL) olive oil

2 tbsp (25 mL) balsamic vinegar

½ tsp (2 mL) salt

1½ cups (375 mL) freshly grated Parmesan cheese

In small bowl, combine parsley, garlic and hot pepper flakes. Trim mushrooms and brush off any dirt with damp cloth.

In large bowl, whisk together oil, vinegar and salt. Add mushrooms. Toss to coat lightly.

Spread mushrooms in single layer on baking sheet. Sprinkle with parsley mixture and Parmesan.

Cook in preheated 400 F (200 C) oven about 10 minutes or until just tender. Place on serving platter with juices.

*Makes 4 to 6 servings.*

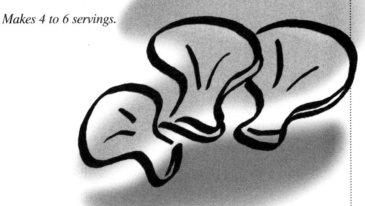

This amazing down-home Italian dish – basically, roasted mushrooms – is from Eugenia Barato, chef and owner with her husband, Tony, one of the best restaurants in Toronto's Little Italy, Trattoria Giancarlo. This dish is so popular that customers complained bitterly when she once took it off the menu – so there it stays.

If you are using the meaty portobello mushrooms, slice them so that they take the same time to cook as the other mushrooms. Serve this with crusty bread for mopping up the delicious juices, either as an appetizer or as a side dish with roast meat or fish.

# RATATOUILLE

*6 tbsp (75 mL) olive oil*

*4 medium zucchini, quartered and cut in cubes*

*Salt to taste*

*1 sweet yellow pepper, cut in cubes*

*1 sweet red pepper, cut in cubes*

*1 large eggplant or 6 Japanese eggplants, unpeeled, cut in cubes*

*Freshly ground black pepper*

*1 large red onion, cut in cubes*

*2 large cloves garlic, finely chopped*

*1 tbsp (15 mL) chopped fresh thyme, oregano or herbes de provence, or ½ tsp (2 mL) dried*

*3 ripe tomatoes, peeled, seeded and coarsely chopped (page 71)*

Heat 1 tbsp (15 mL) oil in large skillet over medium-high heat. Add zucchini; sprinkle lightly with salt. Cook, stirring occasionally, about 5 minutes or until golden. Transfer to ovenproof dish with lid or Dutch oven.

Heat 1 tbsp (15 mL) oil in skillet. Add peppers and cook about 5 minutes. Add to zucchini in ovenproof dish.

Heat 3 tbsp (45 mL) oil in skillet. Add eggplant and cook about 5 minutes or until browned and slightly softened. Sprinkle with salt and pepper. Stir into zucchini mixture.

Heat remaining oil in skillet over medium heat. Add onion, garlic and thyme. Cook, stirring, about 4 minutes or until softened. Add tomatoes. Cook about 10 minutes or until they form a thick sauce. Season with salt and pepper. Pour over vegetables in ovenproof dish but do not stir.

Cover and bake in preheated 350 F (180 C) oven 20 minutes. Remove cover and cook about 15 minutes or until vegetables are tender but not mushy. Baste top with juices forming at bottom of pan once or twice.

Serve warm, at room temperature or chilled.

*Makes 4 to 6 servings.*

*Y*ou can cut the vegetables into round slices or julienne strips for this wonderful summer dish. I developed this version after thoroughly researching different methods for preparing ratatouille and finding that you get the best results by sautéing each vegetable separately before cooking them all together in the oven. You could also brush the vegetables lightly with olive oil and grill them on the barbecue or under the broiler instead of sautéing them.

This dish makes very versatile leftovers. Chop leftover ratatouille and serve it with crackers or crostini as a dip, layer it between noodles in lasagna or between grated cheese and cooked polenta for a fabulous casserole.

I like to cut the vegetables into ½-inch (1 cm) to 1-inch (2.5 cm) cubes for this dish; and I nearly always crumble goat cheese over my finished ratatouille and brown it quickly under the broiler for a delectable, tangy topping.

# HERBED GRILLED VEGETABLES

½ cup (125 mL) chopped fresh chervil or basil

¼ cup (50 mL) chopped fresh chives or green onions

¼ cup (50 mL) chopped fresh parsley

1 tbsp (15 mL) chopped fresh tarragon

2 anchovies, rinsed and chopped (optional)

1 tbsp (15 mL) capers, chopped

2 cloves garlic, finely chopped

Finely grated rind of 1 lemon

1 cup (250 mL) olive oil

½ tsp (2 mL) freshly ground black pepper

6 Japanese eggplants, ends trimmed,
or equivalent amount of other veggies

Juice of 1 lemon

Salt and freshly ground black pepper to taste

In bowl, combine chervil, chives, parsley, tarragon, anchovies (if using), capers, garlic, lemon rind, olive oil and pepper.

Cut eggplants lengthwise into slices ¼ inch (.5 cm) thick. Grill 3 to 4 minutes per side or until slightly charred and soft to touch, basting with herb mixture at intervals.

Transfer to warm serving platter. Drizzle with lemon juice and sprinkle with salt and pepper. Serve any remaining herb mixture on side.

*Makes 4 to 6 servings.*

*The* basting sauce used here would be ideal for almost any grilled food, including bread. Chervil is a delicate herb that adds a unique flavour to this dish. It is worth searching out at a gourmet grocery store, but you can use basil instead. This works particularly well on eggplant but would also work with zucchini, peppers, onions and other veg.
You could make a tasty sauce to drizzle over these at serving time by blending some soft goat cheese with a little cream (whipping or half-and-half), chopped fresh herbs, salt and pepper.

# SKILLET VEGGIES

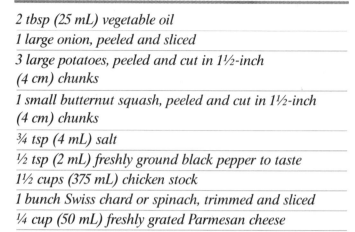

*This is a nifty way to cook almost any vegetable. You could also roast the veggies (except for the chard and spinach) by following my method which is a combination of steaming and roasting, all done in the oven.*

*2 tbsp (25 mL) vegetable oil*

*1 large onion, peeled and sliced*

*3 large potatoes, peeled and cut in 1½-inch (4 cm) chunks*

*1 small butternut squash, peeled and cut in 1½-inch (4 cm) chunks*

*¾ tsp (4 mL) salt*

*½ tsp (2 mL) freshly ground black pepper to taste*

*1½ cups (375 mL) chicken stock*

*1 bunch Swiss chard or spinach, trimmed and sliced*

*¼ cup (50 mL) freshly grated Parmesan cheese*

Heat oil in large skillet over medium heat. Add onion and cook about 20 minutes, stirring occasionally, until deep golden-brown. Stir in potatoes and squash. Sprinkle with salt and pepper. Pour chicken stock over. Bring to a boil, reduce heat and cook, covered, about 15 minutes or until vegetables are just tender. Uncover and simmer about 15 minutes or until most of liquid has evaporated. Stir in Swiss chard. Cover and simmer 5 minutes.

Sprinkle Parmesan over vegetables. Place under broiler about 2 minutes, if desired, to melt cheese.

*Makes 6 to 8 servings.*

## Roasted Veggies

Use large chunks or medium florets of veggies such as (in my order of preference) potatoes, squash, cauliflower, fennel, parsnips, rutabagas, onions and beets. Toss in large bowl with favourite herbs, salt, pepper and olive oil. Transfer to roasting pan and arrange in single layer. Add a little water to pan and cover. Roast in preheated 400 F (200 C) oven 20 minutes. Remove cover and roast 15 to 20 minutes longer or until crisp and nicely browned.

# CURRIED CHICKPEAS

2 tbsp (25 mL) vegetable oil

2 large onions, chopped

3 cloves garlic, finely chopped

1 tbsp (15 mL) finely chopped fresh ginger root

2 tsp (10 mL) ground cumin

2 tsp (10 mL) ground coriander

½ tsp (2 mL) salt

¼ tsp (1 mL) cayenne pepper

¼ tsp (1 mL) turmeric

19-oz (540 mL) can tomatoes, undrained, chopped

Two 19-oz (540 mL) cans chickpeas, drained and rinsed

½ tsp (2 mL) garam masala

1 tbsp (15 mL) cider vinegar or wine vinegar

2 tbsp (25 mL) chopped fresh coriander or parsley

Heat oil in large saucepan over medium heat. Add onions. Cook, stirring occasionally, 5 minutes or until softened. Stir in garlic, ginger, cumin, ground coriander, salt, cayenne and turmeric. Cook, stirring, about 2 minutes or until spices are fragrant. Stir in tomatoes and chickpeas. Bring to a boil, reduce heat and simmer about 10 minutes or until sauce is slightly thickened. Stir in garam masala and vinegar. Cook 2 minutes. Sprinkle with fresh coriander.

*Makes 4 to 6 servings.*

Serve this delectable, nutritious curry over rice along with traditional accompaniments such as mango chutney and raita (page 47). It can also be served at room temperature as part of a potluck or buffet meal. Garam masala is available in East Indian shops and specialty spice stores. If you are using home-cooked chickpeas, you'll need about 5 cups (1.25 L).

# Best Baked Beans

*I came back from a food conference in Boston inspired to make these, an especially appropriate dish for Ontario, where we grow plenty of the right beans. Made with maple syrup, this is a particularly Canadian version of a wonderful winter standby. If you want to make a meatless version, add 2 tbsp (25 mL) tomato paste along with the molasses mixture instead of using salt pork or bacon.*

| |
| --- |
| 2 cups (500 mL) dried pea (navy) beans (1 lb/500 g) |
| 6 oz (175 g) salt pork, thinly sliced, or 4 slices bacon, chopped |
| 1 onion, chopped |
| 2 cloves garlic, finely chopped |
| ½ cup (125 mL) molasses |
| ¼ cup (50 mL) maple syrup or brown sugar |
| 1 tsp (5 mL) ground ginger |
| 1 tsp (5 mL) dry mustard |
| ½ tsp (2 mL) dried thyme |
| 3 cups (750 mL) boiling water |
| 1 tsp (5 mL) salt, or to taste |

Soak beans in plenty of cold water overnight. (Or, for a quick soak, bring beans and water to a boil; turn off heat and let beans stand 1 hour.) Drain.

In small saucepan, cover salt pork with water. Bring to a boil, reduce heat and simmer 10 minutes. Drain. (If using bacon, omit this step.)

In large, ovenproof Dutch oven, place half the beans. Top with salt pork or bacon, onion, garlic and remaining beans.

In bowl, combine molasses, maple syrup, ginger, mustard, thyme and boiling water. Stir to dissolve molasses. Pour over beans; do not stir.

Cook, covered, in preheated 300 F (150 C) oven 5 to 6 hours or until beans are tender and liquid is deep-brown. Stir in salt. Cook 30 minutes longer.

*Makes 6 to 8 servings.*

# LOW-FAT GARLIC MASHED POTATOES

*2 lb (1 kg) potatoes, peeled and cubed (4 to 6)*

*8 cloves garlic, peeled and crushed*

*1 tsp (5 mL) salt*

*½ cup (125 mL) vegetable or chicken stock*

*¼ cup (50 mL) buttermilk (page 171), plain yogurt or low-fat sour cream*

*Pinch freshly ground black pepper*

*Pinch grated nutmeg*

*1 tbsp (15 mL) finely chopped chives or green onions*

In large saucepan, combine potatoes, garlic and salt and cover with cold water. Bring to a boil, reduce heat and simmer about 15 minutes or until tender. Drain.

Return potatoes and garlic to saucepan and place over low heat about 1 minute to dry slightly. Mash potatoes by hand with fork or potato masher, or put through ricer or food mill. Stir in stock, buttermilk, pepper, nutmeg and chives.

*Makes 4 servings.*

## Roasted Garlic

Slice about ¼ inch (.5 cm) off the top of a whole unpeeled garlic bulb. Wrap bulb in foil and bake in preheated 350 F (180 C) oven about 45 minutes or until soft. Squeeze cooked garlic cloves out of skins.

◆

*Y*ou can use roasted garlic instead of raw garlic in this recipe - mash the roasted garlic cloves along with the potatoes. You could also replace half the potatoes with rutabaga and/or a couple of parsnips for a tasty change. Or try using soft goat cheese instead of half the buttermilk.
I like to use Yukon Gold potatoes for their buttery look and smooth texture.

◆

# PERSIAN JEWELLED RICE

*1 cup (250 mL) dried barberries*

*Thinly sliced rind of 2 oranges*

*2 carrots, peeled and cut in thin strips*

*1 cup (250 mL) granulated sugar*

*3 cups (750 mL) raw basmati rice*

*2 tbsp (25 mL) salt*

*1 tsp (5 mL) saffron threads,*
*or ½ tsp (2 mL) ground saffron*

*½ cup (125 mL) butter, melted*

*2 tbsp (25 mL) plain yogurt*

*1 tsp (5 mL) Persian allspice*

*1 onion, thinly sliced*

*½ cup (125 mL) raisins*

*2 tbsp (25 mL) slivered almonds*

*2 tbsp (25 mL) slivered pistachios*

Persia, now known as Iran, is home to some of the finest rice dishes in the world. This one, a classic, was inspired by cookbook author and Persian cooking pro now living in the United States, Najmieh Batmangli. It has a caramelized crust on the bottom, is laden with contrasts in taste, colour and texture and is well worth the slightly tricky cooking method for the amazing results. I discovered this aromatic creation when I was writing about the Iranian New Year, *Nowruz*, which is celebrated in the spring. Barberries, Persian allspice, saffron and slivered pistachios can be found at Iranian and specialty food stores. Substitute dried cranberries or currants for the barberries (a small, tart red berry known in Iran as *zereshk*) in a pinch. Instead of Persian allspice (sometimes referred to as rice spice), you could use regular allspice, ground cumin, or a combination of ½ tsp (2 mL) ground cardamom and ¼ tsp (1 mL) each ground cumin and ground cinnamon. For a lower-fat version of this dish, you could use less butter; you could also use olive oil instead of butter. I would serve this with a hearty stew, spicy curry, tandoori chicken (page 70) or perhaps grilled meat or fish.

Remove and discard stems from barberries. Cover berries with cold water and soak 20 minutes. Drain and rinse well.

In medium saucepan, cover orange rind with cold water. Bring to a boil; drain.

Return rind to saucepan along with carrots, sugar and 1 cup (250 mL) water. Bring to a boil, reduce heat and simmer 10 minutes; drain.

In large saucepan, bring 8 cups (2 L) water to a boil.

Meanwhile, place rice in bowl and cover with warm water; drain. Repeat 4 times.

Add rice and salt to boiling water in large saucepan. Stir, reduce heat and simmer about 10 minutes or until rice is just tender. Drain.

In small bowl, dissolve saffron in ¼ cup (50 mL) hot water.

Heat 2 tbsp (25 mL) butter in large, heavy-bottomed saucepan over low heat.

In medium bowl, combine 2½ cups (625 mL) parcooked rice with yogurt and a few drops of saffron water. Spread mixture over butter in saucepan. (This layer will form the crust.) Add half of remaining parcooked rice to saucepan and top with half orange rind mixture. Sprinkle with ½ tsp (2 mL) allspice.

Repeat layers with remaining ingredients, forming pyramid shape (which allows rice to expand), ending with allspice. Cover and cook over low heat 10 minutes.

Pour remaining saffron mixture and 2 tbsp (25 mL) butter

over rice. Place clean dish towel over saucepan and top with lid. Cook 45 minutes over very low heat. Place covered saucepan on damp folded tea towel 5 minutes to loosen rice crust from bottom of pan.

Heat remaining butter in small skillet over medium heat. Add onion. Cook about 5 minutes or until very tender. Stir in barberries and raisins. Cook about 1 minute.

To serve, spoon half of cooked rice onto serving platter followed by half of barberry mixture. Repeat layers with remaining ingredients to form a mound. Sprinkle with almonds and pistachios.

With spatula, carefully scrape rice crust from bottom of saucepan and serve separately on small plate.

*Makes 8 servings.*

# ROASTED BALSAMIC POTATOES

*1½ lb (750 g) small red potatoes, scrubbed and quartered*

*2 onions, peeled leaving root end intact, cut in wedges*

*2 tbsp (25 mL) olive oil*

*¼ cup (50 mL) balsamic vinegar*

*1 tbsp (15 mL) chopped fresh thyme, or ½ tsp (2 mL) dried*

*½ tsp (2 mL) salt*

*¼ tsp (1 mL) freshly ground black pepper*

*A* delectable, easy way to cook my favourite veg – the lowly spud. This works best with those small red potatoes that are best cooked in their skins. The trick is that secret ingredient no kitchen should be without – balsamic vinegar.

In 13 x 9-inch (3 L) baking dish, combine potatoes, onions and oil. Cover and bake in preheated 400 F (200 C) oven 30 minutes.

Add balsamic vinegar, thyme, salt and pepper, stirring to coat potatoes well. Increase oven temperature to 450 F (230 C).

Bake, uncovered, 30 to 40 minutes, stirring twice, until liquid has evaporated and potatoes are crisp at edges.

*Makes 4 servings.*

# Carib Squash Dumplings

When chef Steven Potovsky worked at The Rivoli, he served this dish at one of the fabulous fundraisers designed to raise money for Second Harvest. He used Jamaican ingredients such as calabeza squash (Jamaican pumpkin), escallions (Jamaican green onions) and callaloo leaves (Jamaican spinach) for his version. These ingredients are available at the Kensington Market and other Caribbean food stores. Our slightly simplified version uses easy-to-find ingredients; it makes a fabulous meatless dish to serve as an appetizer or side dish.

## Dumplings:

*1 small butternut squash (1 lb/500 g), peeled and cut in 1-inch (2.5 cm) chunks*

*1 egg*

*1 large green onion, chopped*

*½ tsp (2 mL) ground allspice*

*½ tsp (2 mL) salt*

*¼ tsp (1 mL) dried thyme*

*¼ tsp (1 mL) dried oregano*

*1 cup (250 mL) all-purpose flour*

*2 tbsp (25 mL) olive oil*

## Sauce:

*1 tbsp (15 mL) olive oil*

*1 onion, chopped*

*2 cloves garlic, finely chopped*

*½ tsp (2 mL) hot pepper flakes*

*1 tbsp (15 mL) curry powder, or to taste*

*1 cup (250 mL) coconut milk*

*½ cup (125 mL) dark ale*

*2 cups (500 mL) chopped fresh spinach*

*1 large tomato, chopped*

*½ tsp (2 mL) salt*

*4 green onions, chopped*

*½ cup (125 mL) chopped fresh coriander or parsley*

In large saucepan, steam or boil squash about 15 minutes or until very tender. Drain. Cool completely in colander to remove excess moisture.

In food processor, combine squash, egg, green onion, allspice, salt, thyme and oregano, pulsing with on/off motion and scraping down sides of bowl until smooth. Add flour, mixing just until blended.

Drop batter by large spoonfuls into large saucepan of boiling, salted water, about 12 at a time. Cook about 3 minutes or until dumplings rise to surface of water. Remove from saucepan with slotted spoon. Toss gently with oil to prevent sticking.

To prepare sauce, heat oil in large saucepan over medium

heat. Add onion, garlic and hot pepper flakes. Cook about 4 minutes or until softened. Stir in curry powder. Cook 1 minute. Add dumplings, stirring gently to coat with spices. Add coconut milk, ale, spinach, tomato and salt. Bring to a boil, reduce heat and simmer about 7 minutes or until spinach has wilted. Stir in green onions and half of coriander.

Serve in bowls garnished with remaining coriander.

*Makes 4 servings.*

# SQUASH POTATO GRATIN

*½ medium butternut squash, peeled and cubed (4 cups/1 L)*

*4 large potatoes, peeled and cubed*

*2 tbsp (25 mL) olive oil*

*1 large onion, coarsely chopped*

*2 eggs*

*1 cup (250 mL) shredded Gruyère cheese (4 oz/125 g)*

*½ tsp (2 mL) grated nutmeg*

*Salt and freshly ground black pepper to taste*

*1 tbsp (15 mL) butter*

*1 cup (250 mL) fresh soft breadcrumbs*

Place squash and potatoes in large heavy saucepan. Add enough water to cover and bring to a boil. Reduce heat and simmer, covered, about 20 minutes or until soft. Drain.

Meanwhile, coat 13 x 9-inch (3 L) baking dish or ovenproof casserole with olive oil. Spread onion in dish.

Bake in preheated 400 F (200 C) oven 10 to 15 minutes or until onion is browned.

Drain squash/potato mixture and transfer to large bowl. Add eggs and ¾ cup (175 mL) cheese. Mix together, then mash with potato masher or hand mixer. Stir in nutmeg, salt and pepper.

Spread mixture over onions in baking dish, smoothing top.

Melt butter in small saucepan. Stir in breadcrumbs. Sprinkle over squash mixture. Sprinkle remaining cheese on top.

Return to oven and bake, uncovered, about 30 minutes or until golden-brown.

*Makes 6 to 8 servings.*

*Y*ou could use any kind of winter squash for this – butternut, hubbard, acorn or even pumpkin. It's the perfect side dish to make ahead for a Thanksgiving or other fall/winter meal – tasty, nutritious and elegantly homey. I often take it to potlucks baked in an attractive earthenware dish. You could use Cheddar instead of Gruyère cheese if desired, but use only homemade breadcrumbs; they're easily made by whirring stale bread in the food processor.

# WHEAT BERRY BARLEY RISOTTO

½ cup (125 mL) wheat berries

½ cup (125 mL) pearl barley

1 tbsp (15 mL) olive oil

1 clove garlic, finely chopped

½ cup (125 mL) diced zucchini

½ cup (125 mL) corn kernels

½ cup (125 mL) chopped tomatoes

Pinch grated nutmeg

Salt and freshly ground black pepper to taste

## RISOTTO:

4 to 5 cups (1 to 1.25 L) vegetable or chicken stock

1 tbsp (15 mL) olive oil

1 tbsp (15 mL) butter

1 onion, chopped

1 clove garlic, finely chopped

½ cup (125 mL) raw Arborio rice

½ cup (125 mL) dry white wine

A few saffron threads (optional)

1 tbsp (15 mL) chopped fresh thyme,
or ½ tsp (2 mL) dried

Salt and freshly ground black pepper to taste

## GARNISH:

1 tsp (5 mL) butter

2 tbsp (25 mL) freshly grated Parmesan cheese

1 green onion, chopped

This elegant, flavourful and healthy dish is made using the traditional risotto method, but with a few inventive twists. It comes from Mark McEwan, ace chef/owner of upscale north Toronto eatery, North 44, who introduced me to wheat berries – unhulled wheat kernels sold in most health-food stores.
If you are using canned or cubed stock in this, wait until the end of cooking before adding any salt, as these products have a higher salt content than homemade stock. Toasting the barley adds a lovely nutty flavour. Use Arborio, a special short-grain Italian rice.

Rinse wheat berries.  Place in bowl and cover with cold water. Soak at least 6 hours or overnight. Drain well.

Place berries in large saucepan with enough cold water to cover by at least a couple of inches. Bring to a boil, reduce heat and simmer over low heat 1½ hours or until tender but not soft.

Meanwhile, in heavy skillet over medium heat, toast barley about 8 minutes or until fragrant. Cool.

Heat oil in large, heavy saucepan. Add garlic, zucchini and corn.  Cook 2 minutes. Stir in tomatoes and cook 1 minute longer. Add nutmeg, salt and pepper. Remove vegetables to platter.

For risotto, bring stock to boil in separate saucepan. Reduce heat to medium and let simmer as you prepare risotto.

In saucepan used for vegetables, heat oil and butter over medium heat. Add onion and garlic. Cook, stirring, about 4 minutes or until softened. Add toasted barley and rice. Cook 1 minute. Stir in wheat berries. Pour in wine and cook until evaporated, about 2 to 3 minutes.

Add about ½ cup (125 mL) simmering stock. Increase heat to medium-high so liquid maintains a brisk boil. Stir in saffron (if using), thyme, salt and pepper. Cook, stirring constantly, until liquid has almost been absorbed. Continue adding simmering stock ½ cup (125 mL) at a time, stirring well after each addition to prevent rice from sticking, about 10 minutes.

Stir in vegetables. Keep adding stock until all grains are tender but firm to the bite, 10 to 15 minutes more.

For garnish, stir in butter, Parmesan and green onion. Taste and adjust seasoning.

*Makes 4 to 6 servings.*

# Couscous with Unusual Greens

*8 oz (250 g) fresh dill (1 large bunch) or fennel leaves or a combination, roots and tough stems removed*

*8 oz (250 g) fresh parsley leaves*

*1 bunch green onions, trimmed*

*2 large leeks, white part only*

*½ cup (125 mL) tightly packed celery leaves*

*½ cup (125 mL) tightly packed carrot tops*

*¼ cup (50 mL) olive oil*

*1 large onion, chopped*

*6 cloves garlic, finely chopped*

*3 tbsp (45 mL) tomato paste*

*1 tbsp (15 mL) paprika*

*2 tsp (10 mL) salt*

*1 tsp (5 mL) ground coriander*

*1 tsp (5 mL) ground caraway seeds*

*½ tsp (2 mL) hot pepper flakes*

*1 sweet red pepper, cut in strips 1 inch (2.5 cm) wide*

*2½ cups (625 mL) quick-cooking couscous*

Wash dill, parsley, green onions, leeks, celery leaves and carrot tops thoroughly. Place in steamer basket over boiling water. Steam 30 minutes. Cool slightly and chop coarsely.

Heat oil in large skillet over medium heat. Add onion and cook, stirring occasionally, about 4 minutes or until softened. Stir in garlic and tomato paste. Cook about 3 minutes, stirring, until paste has dissolved. Add paprika, salt, coriander, caraway and hot pepper flakes. Cook, stirring, about 2 minutes. Stir in 1 cup (250 mL) water, steamed greens and red pepper strips. Reduce heat to low, cover and cook 20 minutes.

Meanwhile, in large saucepan, bring 3½ cups (875 mL) water to a boil. Stir in couscous. Let simmer about 1 minute or until water has almost been absorbed. Cover and remove from heat. Let stand 5 minutes. Fluff with a fork. Gently mix couscous with greens until well combined.

*Makes 8 servings.*

*I* am a shameless recipe mooch; my justification is that one has to be in my job. I got wind of this one at the Association of Food Journalists conference in Atlanta one year, when Nancy McKeown, food editor at the *Washington Post*, told me she had spent hours making this dish – with divine results. We tried the recipe and hereby confirm that she was right on both counts. You could use spinach, kale or Swiss chard instead of the carrot tops and celery leaves. Quick-cooking couscous is sold in major supermarkets and bulk-food stores as well as in Middle Eastern and gourmet food shops. We found it necessary to measure the dill and parsley by weight since the bunches vary so much in size. Use a blender or coffee mill to grind the spices. This dish takes a bit of work – both in the shopping and the cooking – but it is well worth it.

# Breakfasts, Brunches and Breads

## OVEN-BAKED BANANA FRENCH TOAST

I've had a soft spot for French toast ever since I was a kid, when my dad used to make it on Sundays. Here's a yummy, souped-up version ideal for a lazy weekend breakfast or holiday brunch. Serve it with maple syrup or your favourite low-fat topping such as slightly sweetened plain yogurt. Don't use over-ripe bananas; they get too mushy when cooked. We used a 1-lb (500 g) challah (Jewish egg bread) for this, but you could also use raisin or whole wheat bread.

| |
|---|
| 3 eggs |
| 4 egg whites |
| 1½ cups (375 mL) milk |
| 1 tsp (5 mL) vanilla |
| ½ tsp (2 mL) salt |
| ¼ cup (50 mL) packed brown sugar |
| ½ tsp (2 mL) ground cinnamon |
| 1 loaf egg bread, unsliced |
| 2 bananas, sliced |
| 1 cup (250 mL) chopped walnuts or pecans (4 oz/125 g) |

In large bowl, whisk together eggs, egg whites, milk, vanilla and salt.

In small bowl, combine sugar and cinnamon.

Slice bread into slices 1 inch (2.5 cm) thick. To make each slice into a hinged sandwich, slice again in the same direction almost to the crust, leaving about ½-inch (1 cm) crust attached. Inside each slice, place banana slices in single layer. Sprinkle brown sugar mixture over bananas.

Place in greased 13 x 9-inch (3 L) baking dish. Pour in egg mixture. Let stand 5 minutes. Turn each slice over. Cover with plastic wrap and refrigerate at least 1 hour or overnight.

Remove plastic wrap; sprinkle with nuts. Bake, uncovered, in preheated 350 F (180 C) oven 30 minutes or until golden.

*Makes 8 servings.*

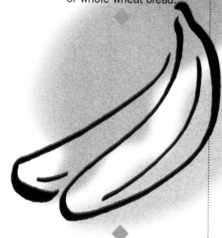

## SKILLET CORNBREAD

This is one of the best cornbreads I've tasted – moist and full of contrasting textures. Great with chili, a hearty soup or served on a buffet at a barbecue, it will disappear in no time. A cast-iron skillet works well for this but you could simply make it in a baking pan.

| |
|---|
| 1 cup (250 mL) cornmeal |
| 1 cup (250 mL) all-purpose flour |
| 2 tbsp (25 mL) granulated sugar |
| 1 tsp (5 mL) baking soda |
| ½ tsp (2 mL) salt |
| ½ tsp (2 mL) ground cumin |
| 14-oz (398 mL) can creamed corn |
| 2 eggs |
| ½ cup (125 mL) buttermilk (page 171) |
| ¼ cup (50 mL) vegetable oil |
| 2 jalapeño peppers, finely chopped (optional) |

In large bowl, combine cornmeal, flour, sugar, baking soda, salt and cumin.

In separate bowl, whisk together creamed corn, eggs, buttermilk, oil and jalapeños (if using). Stir into flour mixture just until all ingredients are moistened.

Pour batter into well-greased 8-inch (20 cm) ovenproof skillet or baking pan. Bake in preheated 400 F (200 C) oven about 30 minutes or until golden on top and toothpick inserted in centre comes out clean. Turn out onto rack to cool slightly. Cut into wedges; serve warm.

*Makes 8 servings.*

# Cottage Cheese Pancakes

| |
|---|
| *1 cup (250 mL) cottage cheese* |
| *2 eggs* |
| *¼ cup (50 mL) whole wheat or all-purpose flour* |
| *2 tbsp (25 mL) wheat bran* |
| *¼ tsp (1 mL) ground cinnamon* |
| *Pinch salt* |

In food processor or blender, combine cottage cheese and eggs, processing until smooth. Transfer to bowl. Stir in flour, bran, cinnamon and salt to form a smooth, thick batter.

On lightly greased skillet over medium heat, drop batter by rounded spoonfuls. Cook about 3 minutes or until bubbles appear on surface. Turn and cook about 2 minutes or until golden.

*Makes 8 to 10 small pancakes.*

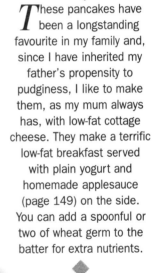

*These pancakes have been a longstanding favourite in my family and, since I have inherited my father's propensity to pudginess, I like to make them, as my mum always has, with low-fat cottage cheese. They make a terrific low-fat breakfast served with plain yogurt and homemade applesauce (page 149) on the side. You can add a spoonful or two of wheat germ to the batter for extra nutrients.*

# Italian Grilled Cheese Sandwich

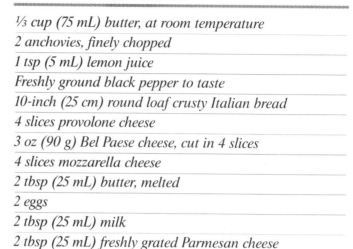

A wonderful baked sandwich from Bar Italia in the heart of Toronto's Little Italy (where it's called Mozzarella in Carrozza). I featured it in an article about the grilled cheese sandwich and its many variations. You could use anchovy paste, available in tubes in some gourmet food shops and supermarkets, instead of anchovy fillets for this delicious breakfast, brunch or light lunch or supper dish. Great with a salad.

⅓ cup (75 mL) butter, at room temperature

2 anchovies, finely chopped

1 tsp (5 mL) lemon juice

Freshly ground black pepper to taste

10-inch (25 cm) round loaf crusty Italian bread

4 slices provolone cheese

3 oz (90 g) Bel Paese cheese, cut in 4 slices

4 slices mozzarella cheese

2 tbsp (25 mL) butter, melted

2 eggs

2 tbsp (25 mL) milk

2 tbsp (25 mL) freshly grated Parmesan cheese

In small bowl, combine butter, anchovies, lemon juice and pinch of pepper until well mixed. Place on waxed paper and roll into 3½ x 1-inch (9 x 2.5 cm) log. Refrigerate 30 minutes or until firm. Cut into 8 slices.

Trim crusts from top and sides of bread. Cut loaf into 4 wedges. Cut each wedge in half horizontally without cutting through back. Open a wedge and scoop out bread on bottom half, leaving ½-inch (1 cm) rim all around.

Place 1 slice anchovy butter in hollow. Top with 1 slice each provolone, Bel Paese and mozzarella. Sprinkle with pepper. Top with another slice of anchovy butter. Close sandwich and repeat with remaining wedges. Brush each sandwich with melted butter.

In small bowl, whisk together eggs and milk. Brush evenly over entire surface of sandwiches. Sprinkle tops with Parmesan. Place on ungreased baking sheet.

Cook in preheated 400 F (200 C) oven 15 to 20 minutes or until golden. Serve each sandwich cut in half.

*Makes 4 servings.*

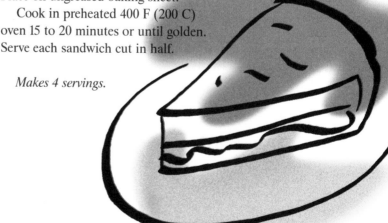

# Springtime Strata

3 eggs

6 egg whites

1¼ cups (300 mL) milk

1 tsp (5 mL) salt

¼ tsp (1 mL) freshly ground black pepper

1 tbsp (15 mL) butter

6 oz (175 g) fresh shiitake, portobello
or button mushrooms, sliced (2 cups/500 mL)

4 green onions, chopped

1 lb (500 g) asparagus, cut in 2-inch (5 cm) lengths

12 slices egg bread, cubed (10 cups/2.5 L)

4 oz (125 g) soft goat cheese, crumbled (¾ cup/175 mL)

¼ cup (50 mL) chopped fresh basil, or 1 tsp (5 mL) dried

In large bowl, whisk together eggs, egg whites, milk, salt and pepper.

Melt butter in skillet over medium-high heat. Add mushrooms and green onions. Cook 5 minutes, stirring occasionally, until tender. Transfer to bowl.

Add asparagus to skillet with 2 tbsp (25 mL) water. Cook about 3 minutes or until asparagus is just tender and water has evaporated.

In greased 12-cup (3 L) shallow casserole or gratin dish, layer half of the bread cubes, half the goat cheese, half the mushroom mixture, half of the asparagus and half the basil. Repeat layers using remaining ingredients.

Pour egg mixture over all, pressing top layer down gently with back of spoon to moisten. Cover and refrigerate at least 3 hours or overnight.

Bake, uncovered, in preheated 350 F (180 C) oven about 1 hour or until puffed and golden. Serve immediately.

*Makes 6 servings.*

You can use low-fat milk to keep the fat content down in this already lighter-than-usual brunch, lunch or light supper dish. It's easily assembled the day ahead and then popped into oven before mealtime. If you can't find fresh asparagus, use snowpeas or broccoli florets. I used almost a whole loaf of braided challah (Jewish egg bread), but whole-wheat or raisin loaf would also work well.

# BROTHER RICK'S ORANGE CRANBERRY BREAD

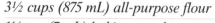

*A* superb quickbread chock-full of goodies, this is from Rick Curry, a Jesuit brother who is an ace baker, author of the jewel of a book, *The Secrets of Jesuit Breadmaking*, and founder of the National Theatre Workshop of the Handicapped in New York City. I tried the recipe when Curry – a congenial fellow and brilliant baker with a great sense of humour – was in town one year to promote his book. It's a winner – ideal for the festive season and for taking as a hostess gift. The cranberries can easily be chopped in the food processor.

*3½ cups (875 mL) all-purpose flour*

*1½ tsp (7 mL) baking powder*

*1 tsp (5 mL) baking soda*

*1 tsp (5 mL) salt*

*½ cup (125 mL) butter, at room temperature*

*1 cup (250 mL) granulated sugar*

*4 tsp (20 mL) finely grated orange rind*

*2 eggs*

*⅔ cup (150 mL) orange juice*

*⅔ cup (150 mL) milk*

*4 oz (120 g) dried apricots, chopped (⅔ cup/150 mL)*

*¾ cup (175 mL) chopped walnuts (3 oz/90 g)*

*3 cups (750 mL) fresh or frozen cranberries, chopped*

In bowl, combine flour, baking powder, baking soda and salt.

In separate large bowl, cream butter, sugar and orange rind until fluffy. Beat in eggs, one at a time, until smooth. Beat in orange juice and milk.

Stir in flour mixture to form a stiff dough. Fold in apricots, walnuts and cranberries just until combined.

Spread batter evenly into 2 greased 8 x 4-inch (1.5 L) loaf pans (or 4 smaller pans). Bake in preheated 350 F (180 C) oven about 1 hour (45 minutes for small loaves) or until toothpick inserted in centre comes out clean. Turn out onto rack to cool completely.

*Makes 2 medium or 4 small loaves.*

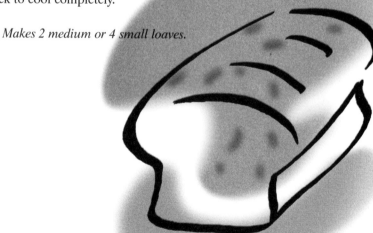

# Scott's Low-Country Grits with Shrimp Paste

## Shrimp Paste:

½ cup (125 mL) butter

8 oz (250 g) shrimp, peeled and deveined

2 tbsp (25 mL) dry sherry

Pinch cayenne pepper

2 tsp (10 mL) lemon juice

Salt to taste

## Grits:

2¼ cups (550 mL) milk

2 cups (500 mL) water

1 cup (250 mL) stone-ground grits

1 tsp (5 mL) salt

1 tbsp (15 mL) butter

For shrimp paste, heat butter in skillet over medium-high heat until foaming.

Add shrimp and cook 3 to 6 minutes (depending on size of shrimp) or just until bright pink. Place shrimp and juices in food processor.

Pour sherry into hot skillet. Cook about 15 seconds, stirring to scrape up brown bits from pan. Pour into food processor with cayenne, lemon juice and salt. Process until smooth. (Shrimp paste can be made up to 2 days ahead. Cover and refrigerate. Reheat very gently over low heat to serve.)

To make grits, bring milk and water to a boil in medium saucepan. Slowly stir in grits and salt. Cover and simmer over low heat about 1 hour, stirring occasionally. Stir in butter.

Serve grits in shallow bowls topped with generous dollops of shrimp paste.

*Makes 6 servings.*

Scott Peacock is one of the top chefs in Atlanta, Georgia. I tried this traditional dish when it was served at a food conference in Atlanta, at a reception showcasing local chefs. This old-fashioned, tasty cereal can be served as a side dish with stew or as part of a Southern-style breakfast. Not for those counting cholesterol, but absolutely delicious! Stone-ground grits can be found in some health-food, bulk-food and gourmet stores.

# TOUCH OF GRACE BISCUITS

*I* got this unusual but wonderful recipe from Shirley Corriher, a bright and witty foodie/food scientist who demonstrated this – her grandmother's recipe – at a food conference I once attended in her native Atlanta. Corriher claims that her grandmother gave the biscuits this name because you need "a touch of grace" to work with the wet dough. The results are truly blessed – an amazingly light, delicate biscuit. By the way, the ice-cream scoop works best because the dough (more like a batter) is so runny. Cake and pastry flour is also key.

*2½ cups (625 mL) cake and pastry flour*

*1 tbsp (15 mL) granulated sugar*

*1½ tsp (7 mL) baking powder*

*Pinch baking soda*

*½ tsp (2 mL) salt*

*3 tbsp (45 mL) shortening or lard*

*¾ cup (175 mL) whipping cream*

*½ cup (125 mL) buttermilk (page 171)*

In bowl, combine 1½ cups (375 mL) flour, sugar, baking powder, baking soda and salt.

Using pastry blender, cut in shortening until mixture resembles coarse meal. Stir in cream and buttermilk; dough will be very wet.

Place remaining flour on work surface or plate. Lightly grease ice-cream scoop or large spoon. Scoop dough onto flour one scoop at a time; sprinkle a little flour over top. With floured hands, pick up dough and toss gently back and forth between hands once or twice to remove excess flour.

Place biscuits close together in greased 8 to 9-inch (20 to 23 cm) round baking pan. Repeat with remaining scoops of dough.

Bake in preheated 475 F (240 C) oven about 18 minutes or until golden- brown. Pull biscuits apart and serve warm.

*Makes 8 biscuits.*

# NAAN

3 cups (750 mL) self-rising flour

1 tsp (5 mL) quick-rise yeast

1 tbsp (15 mL) plain yogurt

1 egg, beaten

2 tbsp (25 mL) vegetable oil

1 cup (250 mL) milk, warm

1 tbsp (15 mL) butter, melted

2 tbsp (25 mL) chopped fresh coriander or parsley

In large bowl, mix together flour and yeast.

In small bowl, combine yogurt, egg and oil.

Add yogurt mixture and warm milk to flour mixture. Stir with fork until dough begins to form a ball. Turn onto work surface and knead 2 minutes or until smooth. (Dough should be soft, not sticky. Add up to 2 tbsp/25 mL more flour if dough is too sticky.)

Place dough in large clean bowl and cover with plastic wrap. Let rise 2 to 3 hours or until doubled.

Divide dough into 4 equal pieces. Roll each piece into a ball. Cover loosely with clean tea towel and let stand 10 minutes. Roll each quarter into round ¼ inch (.5 cm) thick.

Preheat cast-iron or non-stick skillet over medium-high heat. Place one round of dough in skillet. Cook 30 seconds or until lightly browned. With uncooked side up, place skillet 4 to 6 inches (10 to 15 cm) under preheated broiler and cook 30 to 60 seconds or until golden. (To cook on barbecue, preheat grill to medium-high. Place dough directly on grill, close lid and cook 30 seconds or until browned. Turn over, close lid and grill 30 seconds or until browned.)

Brush warm naan with melted butter, sprinkle with chopped coriander and wrap in tea towel to keep moist while cooking remaining naan.

*Makes 4 naan.*

*A* tender and light version of the wondrous Indian flatbread from Metro caterer and cook Satya Ramrakha who is literally the "queen of naan" since she makes about 40 kinds! It is superb with an Indian meal but also great with soup or stew. Traditionally made in a tandoori brick oven, this recipe has been adapted to work well in a regular oven. The barbecue method is also a super, easy way to cook the bread. Self-rising flour and quick-rise yeast (it comes in pouches made by Fleischmann's) can be found in most supermarkets. By the way, this bread can be used as a crust for pizza or to make stuffed sandwiches.

# BREAKFAST BARS

*3 tbsp (45 mL) butter, at room temperature*

*½ cup (125 mL) packed brown sugar*

*2 eggs*

*1¾ cups (425 mL) wheat bran*

*1 cup (250 mL) buttermilk (page 171)*

*1 cup (250 mL) all-purpose flour*

*2 tsp (10 mL) baking soda*

*Pinch salt*

*1 cup (250 mL) chopped walnuts*

*¾ cup (175 mL) currants*

*¾ cup (175 mL) dried apricots,
cut in ½-inch (1 cm) pieces*

In large bowl, combine butter, sugar, eggs, bran, buttermilk, flour, baking soda and salt. Beat with electric mixer at medium speed just until mixed. Stir in walnuts, currants and apricots.

Spread batter evenly in greased 13 x 9-inch (3 L) baking pan. Bake in preheated 375 F (190 C) oven about 20 minutes or until edges are browned. Cool completely in pan on rack. Cut into bars. Wrap individually in plastic wrap. Store in refrigerator.

*Makes 16 bars.*

# Cakes and Cookies

# CHOCOLATE APPLE CAKE

*This rich, moist, brownie-like creation can be made in a round pan and cut into wedges or in a rectangular pan and cut into squares. Superb served with crème fraîche (page 149), sweetened yogurt or vanilla ice cream. You could dust the cooled cake with icing sugar, if desired. McIntosh, Golden Delicious, Mutsu, Cortland and Northern Spy apples all work well; so would ripe pears. You could also add 1 cup (250 mL) raisins or toasted nuts or ¼ cup (50 mL) finely chopped crystallized ginger to the batter before baking. When testing for doneness, a tester inserted in the cake will not come out clean due to the chocolate chips; use our method.*

*2 cups (500 mL) all-purpose flour*

*¾ cup (175 mL) cocoa powder*

*2 tsp (10 mL) baking powder*

*½ tsp (2 mL) baking soda*

*½ tsp (2 mL) salt*

*½ cup (125 mL) butter, melted*

*¾ cup (175 mL) buttermilk (page 171)*

*1½ cups (375 mL) granulated sugar*

*2 eggs*

*1 tbsp (15 mL) vanilla*

*4 apples, peeled, cored and shredded (2 cups/500 mL)*

*3 oz (90 g) bittersweet or semisweet chocolate, chopped, or ½ cup (125 mL) semisweet chocolate chips*

In large bowl, combine flour, cocoa, baking powder, baking soda and salt.

In small bowl, whisk together melted butter, buttermilk, sugar, eggs and vanilla. Pour into flour mixture and stir until well combined. Fold in apples and chocolate. Pour into greased 10-inch (25 cm) springform pan.

Bake in preheated 350 F (180 C) oven about 60 to 70 minutes or until cake springs back when lightly touched and pulls away from sides of pan.

*Makes 10 servings.*

# TRIPLE CHOCOLATE CAKE

⅔ cup (150 mL) slivered almonds

515 g package devil's food chocolate cake mix

113 g package instant chocolate pudding mix

1 cup (250 mL) sour cream or plain yogurt

½ cup (125 mL) vegetable oil

4 eggs

2 tbsp (25 mL) almond or other nut liqueur

½ tsp (2 mL) almond extract

2 cups (500 mL) semisweet chocolate chips
(300 g package)

## CHOCOLATE GLAZE:

4 oz (125 g) bittersweet or semisweet chocolate, chopped

3 tbsp (45 mL) butter

2 tbsp (25 mL) almond or other nut liqueur

1 tsp (5 mL) vegetable oil

Toast almonds in small dry skillet over medium-low heat, stirring frequently, about 7 minutes or until golden.

In large bowl, combine cake mix, pudding mix, sour cream, oil, eggs, liqueur and almond extract. Beat with electric mixer on medium speed 2 minutes. Stir in chocolate chips and ½ cup (125 mL) toasted almonds.

Pour into greased and floured 10-inch (3 L) springform tube pan or Bundt pan. Bake in preheated 350 F (180 C) oven 55 to 60 minutes or until cake springs back when lightly touched and sides begin to pull away from edge of pan. Cool in pan 10 minutes. Remove from pan and invert onto wire rack to cool.

To prepare glaze, in top of double boiler, combine chocolate, butter, liqueur and oil. Place over barely simmering water and stir until chocolate is melted and smooth. Cool slightly. Spoon over cooled cake. Garnish with remaining almonds.

*Makes 12 servings.*

## *Chocolate Sour Cream Icing*

Melt 6 oz (175 g) bittersweet or semisweet chocolate in small saucepan over low heat (or in microwave in small glass dish). Stir in 1 cup (250 mL) sour cream.

*O*ne of those back-of-the-box recipes that should bring even food snobs to their knees. A word of warning, though. Do not answer the phone while making this or the pudding will set and become unmixable. (Thank you to the two readers who inadvertently revealed this hazard when they phoned to tell me this recipe didn't work!) Instead of the glaze used here, this would also be good crowned with Chocolate Sour Cream Icing. In a pinch, you could use brandy, whisky or even coffee in place of liqueur for the Chocolate Glaze.

# DIED-AND-WENT-TO-HEAVEN LIGHT CHOCOLATE CAKE

Thank you to that wonderful magazine, *Eating Well*, for sharing this sublime, low-fat version of chocolate cake with us. Each slice has 4 grams of fat and 222 calories – hard to believe when you savour its delectably rich taste and luscious texture.
If you can, use dark cocoa powder (such as Droste or Poulain) in this cake.

1¾ cups (425 mL) all-purpose flour

1 cup (250 mL) granulated sugar

¾ cup (175 mL) cocoa powder

1½ tsp (7 mL) baking powder

1½ tsp (7 mL) baking soda

1 tsp (5 mL) salt

1¼ cups (300 mL) buttermilk (page 171)

1 cup (250 mL) packed brown sugar

2 eggs, lightly beaten

¼ cup (50 mL) vegetable oil

2 tsp (10 mL) vanilla

1 cup (250 mL) strong hot coffee

## GLAZE:

1 cup (250 mL) icing sugar

½ tsp (2 mL) vanilla

1 to 2 tbsp (15 to 25 mL) buttermilk or low-fat milk

In large bowl, whisk together flour, granulated sugar, cocoa, baking powder, baking soda and salt. Add buttermilk, brown sugar, eggs, oil and vanilla. Beat with electric mixer on medium speed 2 minutes. Whisk in hot coffee. (Batter will be quite thin.) Pour batter into greased and floured 10-inch (3 L) Bundt or tube pan.

Bake in preheated 350 F (180 C) oven 1 hour or until tester inserted in centre comes out clean. Cool on rack 10 minutes. Remove from pan and cool completely.

To prepare glaze, in small bowl, whisk together icing sugar, vanilla and just enough buttermilk to make a thick but pourable glaze.

Set cake on serving plate and drizzle glaze over top.

*Makes 16 servings.*

# COFFEE CAKE

*¼ cup (50 mL) packed brown sugar*

*1 tsp (5 mL) ground cinnamon*

*1 cup (250 mL) butter, at room temperature*

*1¼ cups (300 mL) granulated sugar*

*2 eggs*

*1 cup (250 mL) sour cream or plain yogurt*

*1 tsp (5 mL) vanilla*

*1 tbsp (15 mL) finely grated lemon rind*

*2½ cups (625 mL) cake and pastry flour*

*1½ tsp (7 mL) baking powder*

*1 tsp (5 mL) baking soda*

*½ tsp (2 mL) salt*

*¾ cup (175 mL) fresh or frozen blueberries*

*Icing sugar*

In small bowl, combine brown sugar and cinnamon.

In large bowl, using electric mixer, cream butter and granulated sugar until fluffy. Add eggs one at a time, beating until smooth. Beat in sour cream, vanilla and lemon rind.

In separate bowl, combine flour, baking powder, baking soda and salt. Stir into butter mixture, mixing well until batter is very smooth.

Spread half of batter over bottom of greased and floured 10-inch (3 L) Bundt pan. Sprinkle with half of brown sugar mixture, then half the blueberries. Using fork, gently swirl together layers. Top with remaining batter and sprinkle with remaining brown sugar mixture and blueberries.

Bake in preheated 350 F (180 C) oven about 1 hour or until cake tester inserted in centre comes out clean. Cool in pan 20 minutes. Turn out onto wire rack to cool completely. Dust with sifted icing sugar before serving.

*Makes 12 to 16 servings.*

*A* delicious variation of sour cream coffee cake, the best sweet 'n' simple accompaniment to a cup of tea or coffee that I know. When blueberry season is over, you can substitute fresh chopped cranberries or any other berry or soft fruit. Sliced peaches, nectarines or plums would work well (use about 1 cup/250 mL). Cake and pastry flour gives the cake a lovely, delicate texture. Low-fat sour cream or yogurt would be fine in place of the regular versions.

# UNIONVILLE HOUSE CARROT CAKE

*This comes from Cheryl Ringler, who makes it as a layer cake for her restaurant, Unionville House, on the outskirts of Metro Toronto. It is a delicious carrot cake and great for any occasion, but my recipe tester Heather Epp has made it a few times for weddings, sometimes increasing the amounts for more layers and varying their sizes to make a tiered cake.*

| | |
|---|---|
| *2 cups (500 mL) all-purpose flour* | |
| *2 tsp (10 mL) baking powder* | |
| *2 tsp (10 mL) baking soda* | |
| *2 tsp (10 mL) ground cinnamon* | |
| *1 tsp (5 mL) salt* | |
| *½ tsp (2 mL) grated nutmeg* | |
| *¼ tsp (1 mL) ground allspice* | |
| *4 eggs* | |
| *1¼ cups (300 mL) granulated sugar* | |
| *¼ cup (50 mL) liquid honey* | |
| *1¼ cups (300 mL) vegetable oil* | |
| *3 cups (750 mL) shredded carrots (12 oz/375 g)* | |
| *1 cup (250 mL) crushed pineapple, with juice* | |
| *½ cup (125 mL) shredded coconut (optional)* | |
| *½ cup (125 mL) raisins* | |
| *½ cup (125 mL) chopped walnuts (2 oz/60 g)* | |

## CREAM CHEESE ICING:

*1 lb (500 g) cream cheese, at room temperature*
*1 cup (250 g) butter, at room temperature*
*3 tbsp (45 mL) liquid honey*
*2 tsp (10 mL) vanilla*
*4 cups (1 L) icing sugar, sifted*

In bowl, combine flour, baking powder, baking soda, cinnamon, salt, nutmeg and allspice.

In separate large bowl, using electric mixer, beat together eggs, sugar and honey about 3 minutes or until pale yellow. Add oil and beat 1 minute. Stir in carrots, pineapple, coconut (if using), raisins and walnuts.

Gradually add dry ingredients in three parts, mixing well and scraping down sides of bowl occasionally.

Pour batter into 3 greased and floured 9-inch (23 cm) round baking pans. Bake in preheated 400 F (200 C) oven 5 minutes. Reduce heat to 350 F (180 C) and bake about 25 minutes or until cake tester inserted in centre comes out clean. Cool at least 20 minutes in pans. Turn out onto wire racks and cool completely.

To prepare icing, in bowl, using electric mixer, beat together cream cheese, butter, honey and vanilla until smooth. Gradually beat in icing sugar, adding up to ½ cup (125 mL) more if required for spreading consistency.

Spread icing on top of each cake layer. Stack layers and ice sides. Swirl any remaining icing decoratively on top.

*Makes 16 to 20 servings.*

# Upside-down Cake

2 tbsp (25 mL) butter, melted

¼ cup (50 mL) maple syrup or brown sugar

14-oz (398 mL) can pineapple slices, with ½ cup (125 mL) reserved juice

16 maraschino cherries or pecan halves (optional)

1¼ cups (300 mL) all-purpose flour

1 tsp (5 mL) baking powder

½ tsp (2 mL) baking soda

¼ tsp (1 mL) salt

½ cup (125 mL) butter, at room temperature

¾ cup (175 mL) granulated sugar

2 eggs

1 tsp (5 mL) vanilla

Combine melted butter and maple syrup in bottom of 9-inch (23 cm) square or round baking pan. Place pineapple slices decoratively to cover bottom of pan. Place cherries (if using) in spaces between fruit.

In bowl, combine flour, baking powder, baking soda and salt.

In separate large bowl, cream butter and sugar until fluffy. Beat in eggs one at a time. Add vanilla.

Stir flour mixture into large bowl alternately with reserved pineapple juice, mixing until smooth. Pour over fruit.

Bake in preheated 350 F (180 C) oven about 40 minutes or until cake springs back when lightly touched. Cool 10 minutes and invert onto platter.

*Makes 6 servings.*

You can use several kinds of fruit in this versatile, old-fashioned and delectable dessert. Instead of the pineapple, try using about 10 Italian purple plums, halved, and ½ cup (125 mL) apple juice for the liquid. Even bananas work – use ½ cup (125 mL) apple juice for the liquid and about 3 sliced large bananas. Delicious served warm with crème fraîche (page 149), a little plain yogurt or good-quality vanilla ice cream.

# Queen Elizabeth Cake

*1 cup (250 mL) chopped dates*

*1 cup (250 mL) boiling water*

*1 tsp (5 mL) baking soda*

*¼ cup (50 mL) butter, at room temperature*

*1 cup (250 mL) granulated sugar*

*1 tsp (5 mL) vanilla*

*1½ cups (375 mL) cake and pastry flour*

*1 tsp (5 mL) baking powder*

*¼ tsp (1 mL) salt*

*½ cup (125 mL) chopped walnuts (optional)*

## Topping:

*¼ cup (50 mL) butter*

*½ cup (125 mL) packed brown sugar*

*½ cup (125 mL) shredded sweetened coconut or chopped walnuts*

*3 tbsp (45 mL) whipping cream or light cream*

In small bowl, combine dates, boiling water and baking soda.

In large bowl, beat together butter, granulated sugar and vanilla with wooden spoon until sugar begins to clump.

In third bowl, stir together flour, baking powder and salt. Add to butter mixture alternately with date mixture to form a smooth batter. Stir in walnuts (if using). Pour batter into greased 9-inch (2.5 L) square baking pan.

Bake in preheated 350 F (180 C) oven about 30 minutes or until cake springs back when lightly touched.

Meanwhile, to prepare topping, melt butter in small saucepan. Add brown sugar, coconut and cream. Bring to a boil, stirring, and remove from heat.

Spread topping evenly over hot, cooked cake. Place under broiler about 2 minutes or until topping is bubbling and slightly browned (watch constantly to keep from burning). Cool and cut into squares.

*Makes 12 to 16 squares.*

*I* gleaned this top-notch recipe from ace chef Catherine Wise, who got it from her grandmother. More proof that some of the best foods are those sweet (and this one's sweet!), simple, tried-and-true favourites.

# FLOURLESS CHICKPEA CAKE

*19-oz (540 mL) can chickpeas, drained and rinsed*

*Finely grated rind and juice of 1 lemon*

*4 eggs*

*1 cup (250 mL) granulated sugar*

*½ tsp (2 mL) baking powder*

*Icing sugar*

In food processor, process chickpeas with lemon rind and 2 tbsp (25 mL) juice until very smooth. Add eggs, sugar and baking powder. Process a few seconds until ingredients are well blended. Pour batter into greased 9-inch (23 cm) springform pan.

Bake in preheated 350 F (180 C) oven about 45 minutes or until cake tester inserted in centre comes out clean. Cool about 15 minutes in pan. Remove sides of pan. Drizzle cake with remaining lemon juice and dust with sifted icing sugar.

*Makes 12 servings.*

## *Easy Raspberry Sauce*

Thaw and purée a 300 g package of frozen raspberries. Strain through a sieve to remove seeds, if desired.

*A* deliciously moist cake ideal for those with allergies to wheat. I featured it in an April Fool's Day article on dishes made with surprise ingredients. This cake, which resembles cheesecake in taste and texture, would be great served with fruit compote or fresh fruit salad. Add chopped crystallized ginger and/or a little powdered ginger to the batter if you like. You could also substitute about ¼ cup (50 mL) orange juice and rind for the lemon. For an elegant presentation, serve with raspberry sauce.

# FRENCH COUNTRY APPLE CAKE

## CRUST:

| | |
|---|---|
| 1 cup (250 mL) butter, at room temperature | |
| 1 cup (250 mL) granulated sugar | |
| 1 tbsp (15 mL) lemon juice | |
| 1 tsp (5 mL) vanilla | |
| 4 egg yolks | |
| 2¾ cups (675 mL) all-purpose flour | |

## FILLING:

*2 lb (1 kg) tart apples, peeled, cored and sliced (about 6)*

*¼ cup (50 mL) granulated sugar*

*3 tbsp (45 mL) butter*

*2 tbsp (25 mL) lemon juice*

*2 tbsp (25 mL) Grand Marnier, orange liqueur
or orange juice*

## GLAZE:

*1 egg, beaten*

To prepare crust, in bowl, cream butter and sugar until fluffy. Beat in lemon juice and vanilla. Add egg yolks, one at a time, beating until smooth. Stir in flour just until dough begins to clump. Press into a ball, wrap in plastic wrap and refrigerate.

Meanwhile, to prepare filling, in saucepan over medium-low heat, combine apples, sugar, butter and lemon juice. Cook about 20 minutes or until apples are tender and juices have almost evaporated. Stir in Grand Marnier. Cool completely. Press two-thirds of dough over bottom and 2 inches (5 cm) up sides of 9-inch (23 cm) springform pan. Pour in filling.

On lightly floured surface, roll remaining dough into 9-inch (23 cm) circle. Place over filling, pressing edges to seal. Brush with beaten egg. Trace lattice pattern on surface with prongs of a fork.

Bake in preheated 350 F (180 C) oven about 50 minutes or until golden. Cool in springform pan on rack.

*Makes 10 servings.*

*A* delicious cross between a pie and a cake, this comes from New Zealand food celebrity Annabel Langbein. My older daughter once made this in high school for a cooking project and impressed herself as well as the teacher. You could add sliced plums to the apples for the last 10 minutes of cooking or sprinkle fresh raspberries over the apple layer before placing the top crust. You could also stir ¼ cup (50 mL) chopped crystallized ginger into the apple mixture before cooking. Be sure to reserve the leftover egg whites for another use (such as meringues or low-fat omelettes). Add more apples if you like a higher cake. I like to use Northern Spy, Cortland or Mutsu apples for this.

# CAPERS' APPLE CAKE

4 apples, peeled, cored and thinly sliced

2 tbsp (25 mL) lemon juice

2 tsp (10 mL) ground cinnamon

½ cup (125 mL) vegetable oil

2 eggs

1 tsp (5 mL) finely grated orange rind

¼ cup (50 mL) unsweetened orange juice

1½ tsp (7 mL) vanilla

1½ cups (375 mL) all-purpose flour

¾ cup (175 mL) granulated sugar

1½ tsp (7 mL) baking powder

½ tsp (2 mL) salt

## BROWN SUGAR GLAZE:

½ cup (125 mL) butter,

½ cup (125 mL) brown sugar

¼ cup (50 mL) whipping cream

*This top-notch recipe is from Shaire Stevenson of Capers, a busy business that caters to hungry actors and crews on movie locations around Metro. This cake is great as is, or with vanilla ice cream.*

In bowl, combine apples, lemon juice and cinnamon.

In large bowl, whisk together oil, eggs, orange rind, orange juice and vanilla until frothy.

In separate bowl, stir together flour, sugar, baking powder and salt. Add to egg mixture, stirring just until ingredients are moistened. Fold in apples, mixing only slightly.

Pour batter into well-greased 9-inch (23 cm) springform pan. Bake in preheated 350 F (180 C) oven 55 to 60 minutes or until cake tester inserted in centre comes out clean. Cool in pan 10 minutes before removing outer rim.

Meanwhile, for glaze, in small saucepan, combine butter, brown sugar and whipping cream. Bring just to a boil, stirring until smooth. While cake is still warm, make small holes all over surface with toothpick or skewer and slowly pour glaze over cake.

*Makes 12 servings.*

# BEST BROWNIES

These are for those who like their brownies fudgey rather than cakey. Definitely the best version of the brownie that we've come up with. The only trick is to bake them for just the right amount of time; it could take from 25 to 30 minutes to achieve the dense, moist, only slightly cakey texture. We found it takes exactly 28 minutes in an accurate oven. Use unsalted butter in this, as salted butter will overpower the other tastes.
Use semisweet chocolate if you can't find bittersweet; the former is just a tad sweeter.
Sweet, simple and easy to make (no creaming of butter and sugar involved and no icing, nuts or other accoutrements needed), I offer one warning. Cut them into small squares or bars – a little of one of these babies goes a long way!

*1 cup (250 mL) unsalted butter*

*3 oz (90 g) unsweetened chocolate*

*3 oz (90 g) bittersweet chocolate*

*1¾ cups (425 mL) granulated sugar*

*1 tsp (5 mL) vanilla*

*4 eggs*

*1¼ cups (300 mL) all-purpose flour*

*½ tsp (2 mL) salt*

Melt butter and chocolate in heavy saucepan, stirring frequently, until smooth. (Or microwave in glass bowl on High for 30 seconds. Stir, then continue to microwave and stir at 30-second intervals until melted and smooth.) Add ¾ cup (175 mL) sugar and vanilla to chocolate mixture. Stir until smooth. Pour into large bowl and cool at least 5 minutes.

In separate bowl, whisk together remaining 1 cup (250 mL) sugar and eggs. Slowly pour half of this mixture into chocolate, stirring until well combined.

With electric mixer, beat remaining egg mixture until pale yellow and thick, 2 to 3 minutes. Gently fold into chocolate mixture.

In small bowl, combine flour and salt. Stir into chocolate mixture until combined. Pour batter into ungreased 9-inch (2.5 L) square cake pan.

Bake in preheated 350 F (180 C) oven 28 minutes. Cool in pan on rack. Refrigerate brownies before cutting into bars or squares.

*Makes about 25 brownies.*

# Nanaimo Bars

## Base Layer:

⅓ cup (75 mL) cocoa powder

½ cup (125 mL) butter

¼ cup (50 mL) granulated sugar

1 egg, beaten

1 tsp (5 mL) vanilla

1½ cups (375 mL) graham cracker crumbs

1 cup (250 mL) shredded coconut

½ cup (125 mL) finely chopped walnuts

2 tbsp (25 mL) finely chopped crystallized ginger
(optional)

## Middle Layer:

½ cup (125 mL) butter, at room temperature

3 tbsp (45 mL) milk

2 tbsp (25 mL) vanilla custard powder

2 cups (500 mL) icing sugar, sifted

## Top Layer:

4 oz (125 g) semisweet chocolate

2 tbsp (25 mL) butter

To prepare base layer, in top of double boiler, melt together cocoa, butter and granulated sugar until smooth. Whisk in egg, cooking just until mixture thickens. Remove from heat. Stir in vanilla, graham crumbs, coconut, walnuts and ginger (if using). Press into lightly greased 8-inch (20 cm) square baking pan. Chill.

To prepare middle layer, in small bowl, beat together butter, milk, custard powder and icing sugar until fluffy. Spread over chilled base. Chill about 30 minutes (or freeze 10 minutes) until set.

To prepare top layer, in double boiler or microwave, melt together chocolate and butter, stirring occasionally, until smooth. Spread over middle layer, covering entire surface. Store in refrigerator until serving. Cut into squares.

*Makes about 2 dozen bars.*

*I* remember the day I first tasted a Nanaimo Bar. It was baked by one of my university pals in Edmonton in about 1966. It was love at first bite.
I got this version of the wondrous confection from my colleague, *Toronto Star* recipe tester Karen Boulton, who unearthed it at the source, Nanaimo, B.C. Bird's custard powder is usually used, but other versions of this tried-and-true ingredient also work well.

# Coconut Butter Tart Squares

*You may think it's hard to improve on that magnificent all-Canadian confection, the butter tart, but when we came up with this (it was one of the recipes accompanying a butter tart taste test), I knew we'd found a winner. A tad easier to make than the more fiddly tart version, these have an almost toffee-like texture.*

*2 cups (500 mL) all-purpose flour*

*⅓ cup (75 mL) granulated sugar*

*1 cup (250 mL) cold butter, cubed*

## Topping:

*¼ cup (50 mL) butter, melted*

*3 eggs, lightly beaten*

*2 cups (500 mL) packed brown sugar*

*½ cup (125 mL) quick-cooking oats*

*3 tbsp (45 mL) all-purpose flour*

*1 tsp (5 mL) baking powder*

*1 tsp (5 mL) vanilla*

*¼ tsp (1 mL) salt*

*½ cup (125 mL) raisins*

*½ cup (125 mL) shredded coconut*

*½ cup (125 mL) chopped pecans (2 oz/60 g)*

In bowl, combine flour and granulated sugar. Using pastry blender, cut in butter until mixture resembles coarse crumbs. Press into ungreased 13 x 9-inch (3 L) baking pan.

Bake in preheated 350 F (180 C) oven about 15 minutes or until golden around edges.

Meanwhile, to prepare topping, in bowl, combine melted butter and eggs. Blend in brown sugar, oats, flour, baking powder, vanilla and salt. Stir in raisins, coconut and pecans. Pour topping over base.

Bake about 20 minutes or until top is golden and springs back when lightly touched. Run knife around edges. Cool completely on rack before cutting into squares.

*Makes 2 dozen squares.*

# TOFFEE ALMOND SLICES

*About 30 graham crackers*

*1 cup (250 mL) butter*

*1 cup (250 mL) packed brown sugar*

*1 cup (250 mL) sliced almonds (8 oz/250 g)*

Place graham crackers on baking sheet in single layer with edges touching.

In small saucepan over medium heat, combine butter and brown sugar. Bring to a boil, stirring constantly. Reduce heat and simmer 2 minutes, stirring, until smooth. Pour over graham crackers to cover completely. Sprinkle evenly with almonds.

Bake in preheated 350 F (180 C) oven about 8 minutes or until edges are deep golden. Let cool on pan about 10 minutes. Cut or break into squares or rectangles and transfer to rack to cool while still warm.

*Makes about 5 dozen cookies.*

This is one of those recipes that has been around for years. My hunch is that it was invented by some savvy home economist trying to promote graham crackers; or it could just have been the brainwave of an ingenious home cook. Whatever their source, these crunchy cookies are great to serve with fruit salad or just to nibble on with a cup of tea or coffee.

# Heather's Hermits

*My trusty recipe tester Heather Epp contributed these superb cookies. I have made them myself several times, much to the delight of my daughter. They're a cinch to put together and are one of the best homemade cookies you'll find – amorphous, mounded confections full of good things.*

*½ cup (125 mL) butter, at room temperature*

*1 cup (250 mL) packed brown sugar*

*2 eggs*

*1½ cups (375 mL) all-purpose flour*

*1 tsp (5 mL) baking soda*

*1 tsp (5 mL) ground cinnamon*

*½ tsp (2 mL) ground allspice*

*¼ tsp (1 mL) ground cloves*

*¼ tsp (1 mL) grated nutmeg*

*¼ tsp (1 mL) salt*

*1 cup (250 mL) raisins*

*1 cup (250 mL) chopped dates*

*1 cup (250 mL) chopped walnuts (4 oz/125 g)*

In large bowl, cream butter and sugar until fluffy. Beat in eggs, one at a time, until smooth.

In separate bowl, combine flour, baking soda, cinnamon, allspice, cloves, nutmeg and salt. Gradually stir into butter mixture to form a soft dough. Stir in raisins, dates and walnuts.

Drop batter by large spoonfuls onto lightly greased baking sheet. Bake in preheated 350 F (180 C) oven 8 to 10 minutes or until lightly browned.

*Makes about 4 dozen cookies.*

# EVERYTHING COOKIES

*1 cup (250 mL) butter, at room temperature*

*1 cup (250 mL) packed brown sugar*

*½ cup (125 mL) granulated sugar*

*3 eggs*

*2 tsp (10 mL) vanilla*

*2 cups (500 mL) all-purpose flour*

*2 cups (500 mL) rolled oats*

*(regular or quick-cooking, not instant)*

*1 tsp (5 mL) baking soda*

*¼ tsp (1 mL) salt*

*2 cups (500 mL) raisins*

*12 oz (375 g) bittersweet or semisweet chocolate, cut in chunks, or 2 cups (500 mL) semisweet chocolate chips*

*1½ cups (375 mL) chopped pecans (6 oz/175 g)*

In large bowl, cream butter, brown sugar and granulated sugar until fluffy. Beat in eggs, one at a time, until smooth. Add vanilla.

In separate bowl, combine flour, oats, baking soda and salt. Stir into butter mixture to form a sticky dough. Stir in raisins, chocolate chunks and pecans.

Form dough into 2½-inch (6 cm) balls; flatten slightly. Place on greased baking sheets 2 inches (5 cm) apart.

Bake in preheated 375 F (190 C) oven about 15 minutes or until golden. Partially cool on baking sheet before lifting onto rack to cool completely.

*Makes about 20 large cookies.*

*I* once wrote a feature on homemade cookies in which I confessed that most of the cookie-baking done *chez moi* is in my dreams. Never mind, I continued, we can all dream, and this is one cookie I shall make when that baking day arrives. You could use chocolate chips (preferably the large ones) instead of chocolate chunks in these amazingly good cookies, but for my taste the chunks are worth the extra effort. In a pinch, you could use walnuts, hazelnuts or almonds instead of pecans. If you make these cookies smaller, you will, of course, get more.

# Rugelach

2 cups (500 mL) all-purpose flour

½ cup (125 mL) cold butter, cubed

8 oz (250 g) cream cheese, at room temperature, cut in chunks

1 egg

## Jam Filling:

½ cup (125 mL) raspberry or apricot jam

½ cup (125 mL) packed brown sugar

½ cup (125 mL) finely chopped walnuts

2 tbsp (25 mL) ground cinnamon

2 tbsp (25 mL) cocoa powder

## Chocolate Filling:

8 oz  (250 g) bittersweet or semisweet chocolate, finely chopped (1 cup/250 mL)

¼ cup (50 mL) granulated sugar

2 tbsp (25 mL) cocoa powder

## Glaze:

1 egg, beaten

¼ cup (50 mL) granulated sugar

*Wondrously chewy little crescents made with a cream cheese dough, these are a tradition on Jewish holidays like Rosh Hashanah and one of my favourite cookies for any occasion. Choose either the jam or chocolate filling. A tad fiddly to make, they're well worth the effort.*

For pastry, place flour in bowl.  Using pastry blender, cut in butter until mixture resembles coarse crumbs. With fork, stir in cream cheese and egg, mixing just until dough forms a ball. Turn out onto work surface and knead gently a few times until smooth. Wrap in plastic wrap and chill at least 2 hours or up to 2 days. (Pastry can also be made in food processor.  Process flour and butter until texture of coarse crumbs. Add cream cheese and egg and pulse until dough forms a ball. Knead and refrigerate as above.)

Divide dough into quarters. On lightly floured work surface, roll one-quarter into circle ⅛ inch (.25 cm) thick (or thinner if possible – the cookies will be crisper).

If using jam filling, spread 2 tbsp (25 mL) jam over entire circle.

In bowl, combine brown sugar, walnuts, cinnamon and cocoa. Sprinkle one-quarter of this mixture over jam.

For chocolate filling, simply combine chopped chocolate, sugar and cocoa. Sprinkle one-quarter of mixture over pastry circle.

Cut pastry round into 12 wedges. Roll up each wedge tightly starting at outside edge. Place on greased baking sheet with tip of pastry on bottom. Gently bend ends to form crescents.

Brush crescents with beaten egg and sprinkle with sugar. Repeat with remaining dough and filling.

Bake in preheated 350 F (180 C) oven about 30 minutes or until deep golden-brown. Remove to rack to cool.

*Makes 4 dozen cookies.*

# PECAN PUFFS

*1 cup (250 mL) pecans*

*1 cup (250 mL) butter, at room temperature*

*¼ cup (50 mL) granulated sugar*

*2 cups (500 mL) all-purpose flour*

*2 tsp (10 mL) vanilla*

*¾ cup (175 mL) icing sugar*

Spread pecans on baking sheet. Toast in preheated 350 F (180 C) oven 7 minutes. Cool and chop in food processor to form rough crumbs.

In bowl, cream butter and sugar until fluffy. Add flour. Stir in vanilla and toasted pecans. Mix well.

Form dough into balls the size of a teaspoon. Place on ungreased baking sheet. Bake 20 to 25 minutes until cookies are golden-brown on bottom. Store in airtight container.

Just before serving, sift icing sugar by pressing through sieve to dust cookies.

*Makes about 3½ dozen cookies.*

*A* delectable shortbread-like cookie that I learned about some years ago from food writer Jane Rodmell, owner of the trendy Rosedale food shop, All The Best Fine Foods. Toasting the nuts gives extra flavour. Keep the cookies stored in an airtight container, and dust with sifted icing sugar just before serving.

# RENÉE'S HAZELNUT BISCOTTI

*1 cup (250 mL) hazelnuts (filberts) (5 oz/150 g)*

*1 cup (250 mL) raisins, soaked in hot water
10 minutes and drained*

*2 tbsp (25 mL) anise seeds*

*Finely grated rind of 2 lemons*

*4 eggs*

*2 tbsp (25 mL) brandy*

*2 tsp (10 mL) vanilla*

*4¼ cups (about 1 L) all-purpose flour*

*1 tbsp (15 mL) baking powder*

*½ tsp (2 mL) salt*

*1 cup (250 mL) butter, at room temperature*

*1½ cups (375 mL) granulated sugar*

A first-class version of the trendy, twice-baked Italian cookie from talented chef Renée Foote. Store the cookies in an airtight container for up to ten days. They also freeze well. The perfect accompaniment to a cup of tea, coffee or sweet dessert wine such as Vin Santo. In this case, dunking is definitely allowed – in fact, it's recommended!

Spread hazelnuts on baking sheet. Toast in preheated 350 F (180 C) oven 8 to 10 minutes or until skins split. Place on clean tea towel and cool slightly. Fold towel in half and rub gently to remove bitter skins from nuts.

In small bowl, combine hazelnuts, raisins, anise and lemon rind.

In separate bowl, whisk together eggs, brandy and vanilla.

In third bowl, combine flour, baking powder and salt.

In large bowl, cream butter and sugar until fluffy. Gradually beat in egg mixture until smooth. Stir in flour mixture to form a soft dough. Add hazelnut mixture, stirring just until combined.

Divide dough into 4 sections. On lightly floured work surface, roll each segment into log 2 inches (5 cm) in diameter. Place on greased baking sheets, 2 logs per sheet, about 4 inches (10 cm) apart.

Bake in preheated 325 F (160 C) oven about 30 minutes or until firm and golden. Let cool on baking sheets 10 minutes. Transfer to cutting board. Increase oven temperature to 350 F (180 C).

Using a serrated knife, cut each log diagonally into slices ¾ inch (2 cm) thick. Lay cookies flat on baking sheets. Return to oven and bake about 25 minutes more or until golden-brown and crisp.

*Makes 4½ dozen biscotti.*

# *Desserts*

# CHOCOLATE MOUSSE

*This is one of my favourite recipes. I got it years ago from a caterer friend, who is one of the best cooks I know. She sometimes makes this in large amounts for parties, but no matter how much she makes, it magically seems to disappear. It has only four ingredients and is a cinch to prepare. Best of all, although it's hardly low-cal, it does have less fat than mousses made with butter and cream. I don't worry about the raw eggs in it but do try to use eggs that are fresh and have been stored properly to minimize the risk of bacteria. You can use chocolate chips but top-quality semisweet or bittersweet chocolate makes this truly superb. I like to chill the mousse in small individual glass dishes or wine glasses before serving.*

| |
|---|
| *12 oz (375 g) semisweet chocolate, cut in small chunks, or 2 cups (500 mL) semisweet chocolate chips* |
| *¾ cup (175 mL) very hot double-strength black coffee* |
| *6 eggs, separated* |
| *2 to 3 tbsp (25 to 45 mL) brandy, Scotch or dark rum* |

Place chocolate in blender or food processor. Pour in hot coffee. Blend until chocolate melts and mixture is smooth. Blend in egg yolks one at a time. Blend in brandy. Transfer mixture to large bowl.

In separate bowl, beat egg whites until soft peaks form. Fold gently into chocolate mixture until no white shows. Chill in individual dishes or one glass bowl.

*Makes 6 servings.*

# CREAMY RICE PUDDING

*385 mL can evaporated skim milk*

*1⅓ cups (325 mL) water*

*½ cup (125 mL) raw short-grain rice*

*2 eggs*

*⅓ cup (75 mL) granulated sugar*

*¼ tsp (1 mL) ground cinnamon*

*½ cup (125 mL) raisins (optional)*

*1 tsp (5 mL) vanilla*

In heavy non-stick saucepan, combine evaporated milk, water and rice. Bring to a boil, stirring constantly. Reduce heat to low, cover and cook 40 minutes.

In small bowl, beat together eggs, sugar and cinnamon. Stir into rice mixture. Add raisins (if using). Cook about 3 minutes or until thickened. Remove from heat and stir in vanilla. Serve warm or at room temperature.

*Makes 4 servings.*

## Tofu Rice Pudding

In food processor, blend 12 oz (375 g) soft tofu (1½ cups/375 mL) with 1 cup (250 mL) soy milk and 3 tbsp (45 mL) liquid honey.

In saucepan, combine tofu mixture with 1 cup (250 mL) cooked rice and ½ cup (125 mL) raisins. Bring to a boil, reduce heat and simmer about 10 minutes or until thickened. Transfer to glass bowl and sprinkle with cinnamon.

*Makes 4 servings.*

From the test kitchens of Nestle who make Carnation Milk comes this creamy, rich-tasting pudding that only gets 9 percent of its calories from fat. An added nutritional bonus is that one serving has as much calcium as ¾ cup (175 mL) milk. You can also make this with brown rice, preferably short-grain. To recycle leftover cooked rice, stir together 2 cups (500 mL) cooked rice (instead of the raw rice used here) with the remaining ingredients. Place in an 8-cup (2 L) casserole dish. Cover and bake in preheated 350 F (180 C) oven about 35 minutes, stirring every 10 minutes, until thickened. This is great served with fruit compote or thawed frozen raspberries and their juice. The Tofu Rice Pudding is great for those with milk allergies.

# Mud Pie

*20 Oreo cookies*

*¼ cup (50 mL) butter, melted*

*4 cups (1 L) coffee ice cream, slightly softened*

*2 tbsp (25 mL) corn syrup*

*4 tsp (20 mL) coffee liqueur, coffee or water*

*4 tsp (20 mL) butter*

*2 oz (60 g) semisweet chocolate, coarsely chopped*

*1 oz (30 g) unsweetened chocolate, coarsely chopped*

*½ cup (125 mL) whipping cream*

*1 tbsp (15 mL) icing sugar*

*¼ tsp (1 mL) vanilla*

*Grated semisweet chocolate for garnish*

In food processor, combine cookies and melted butter, pulsing with on/off motion until mixture resembles coarse crumbs.

Line 9-inch (23 cm) pie plate with foil. Press crumbs into bottom and sides of plate with back of spoon. Freeze 30 minutes. Turn crust out of pie plate. Remove and discard foil. Place crust back in pie plate (this prevents crust from sticking to pie plate when serving).

Spoon ice cream into crust, smoothing top. Freeze 1 hour.

In small saucepan over medium heat, melt together corn syrup, liqueur, butter, semisweet and unsweetened chocolates, stirring until smooth. Cool slightly and spoon over ice cream. Working quickly, spread evenly over pie. Return pie to freezer until glaze hardens. Cover with plastic wrap and keep frozen until serving.

Just before serving, whip cream with icing sugar until soft peaks form; add vanilla. Mound onto pie. Garnish with grated chocolate.

*Makes 10 servings.*

This ice-cream cake is sure to be a hit with kids of all ages, not to mention adults. A great birthday cake for a kids' party. For even more chocolate flavour, use chocolate ice cream or substitute it for half the coffee ice cream.

# TARTE TATIN

*2 cups (500 mL) all-purpose flour*

*1 tsp (5 mL) salt*

*¾ cup (175 mL) cold butter, cubed*

*1 egg yolk*

*¼ cup (50 mL) water*

*6 apples or pears, peeled, halved and cored*

*1 tbsp (15 mL) lemon juice*

*¾ cup (175 mL) granulated sugar*

*2 tbsp (25 mL) water*

*2 tbsp (25 mL) butter*

*Pinch grated nutmeg*

In food processor, combine flour and salt. Add cold butter cubes, processing in pulses until mixture resembles coarse crumbs.

In small bowl, whisk together egg yolk and ¼ cup (50 mL) water. Add to flour mixture, processing just until mixture begins to form a ball. Turn dough out onto work surface and knead gently once or twice to bring it together. Wrap in plastic wrap. Refrigerate about 30 minutes.

Meanwhile, in bowl, toss apples with lemon juice.

Heat large ovenproof skillet over medium heat. Add sugar and 2 tbsp (25 mL) water, stirring until dissolved. Without stirring, allow mixture to simmer about 10 minutes or until beginning to turn golden. Remove from heat and place apples cut side up in a circle around outer edge of pan. Place remaining apples in centre, fitting in as many as possible; dot with 2 tbsp (25 mL) butter and sprinkle with nutmeg. Cook over low heat about 25 minutes or until sugar is deep brown and some of liquid from apples has evaporated. Remove from heat.

On floured surface roll out pastry into a circle about ¼ inch (.5 cm) thick. Place over apples, trimming edges to ½ inch (1 cm) over edge of pan. Tuck outer edge of pastry down around apples.

Place skillet in preheated 375 F (190 C) oven. Bake tart about 30 minutes or until pastry is golden. Let stand 10 minutes.

Place large platter over skillet. Quickly and carefully invert skillet, allowing tart to fall out onto platter. There will be a lot of sauce. Serve warm, cut in wedges.

*Makes 6 servings.*

*A* traditional version of the classic dessert made famous by the Tatin sisters who, goes the story, created it at their inn in France's Loire Valley at the beginning of the century. Instead of making the dough, you could easily substitute the storebought stuff; puff pastry would work especially well. The Tatins made the tart – surely the original upside-down dessert – in a cast-iron skillet using apples. You could use a baking pan and substitute pears – just make sure the pears are ripe. The apples in the original recipe are halved, not sliced, which gives an attractive look to the tart, but you could also cut them into wedges and place them in the pan overlapping. I sometimes add about ½ cup (125 mL) dried apricots and ⅓ cup (75 mL) currants to the apple mixture for extra colour and flavour. Serve this warm or at room temperature with vanilla ice cream, crème fraîche (page 149), whipped cream or sweetened plain yogurt. The perfect dessert to serve guests in the fall during apple and pear season.

# FALL FRUIT CRISPS

*I* am a huge fan of fruit crisps, crumbles and cobblers – all desserts that highlight fabulous fall fruits while adding a crunchy, sweet topping. Use this as a guide to the genre and enjoy!

◆ Use a single fruit or a combination such as apple/pear, apple/berry, peach/plum, rhubarb/berry. Experiment with your favourite spices and toppings.

◆ Use 6 cups (1.5 L) fruit for each crisp, to make 6 servings.

◆ A shallow casserole or baking dish works best for juicy fruit such as peaches, plums, berries and rhubarb, as it allows a little of the liquid to evaporate during cooking, preventing the topping from becoming soggy. Use a shallow 8-cup (2 L) casserole or baking dish for crisps and a 12-cup (3 L) dish for cobblers.

◆ Thickening very juicy fruits is a must – 1 tbsp (15 mL) cornstarch is enough to thicken 6 cups (1.5 L) peaches or rhubarb. Mix it directly into the fruit or combine with a little sugar before stirring it into the fruit.

## GRANOLA TOPPING:

*1 cup (250 mL) granola*

*½ cup (125 mL) all-purpose flour*

*½ cup (125 mL) brown sugar*

*Pinch salt*

*¼ cup (50 mL) butter, melted*

In bowl, combine granola, flour, brown sugar and salt. Pour in butter, tossing with a fork until moistened and crumbly.

## OAT NUT TOPPING:

Double the topping and freeze half for a future crisp. Add ½ cup (125 mL) shredded Cheddar cheese for a delicious twist. Great for apples or pears!

*1 cup (250 mL) rolled oats (not instant)*

*½ cup (125 mL) all-purpose flour*

*½ cup (125 mL) brown sugar*

*½ cup (125 mL) chopped nuts*

*½ tsp (2 mL) ground cinnamon*

*Pinch ground cloves*

*Pinch salt*

*½ cup (125 mL) butter, melted*

In bowl, combine oats, flour, brown sugar, nuts, cinnamon, cloves and salt.

Pour in butter, tossing with fork until crumbly.

## OLD-FASHIONED TOPPING:

*½ cup (125 mL) butter, at room temperature*

*1 cup (250 mL) brown sugar*

*1 cup (250 mL) all-purpose flour*

*1 tsp (5 mL) ground cinnamon*

*Pinch salt*

In bowl, combine butter and brown sugar until creamy. Stir in flour, cinnamon and salt until crumbly.

## COBBLER TOPPING:

This cakey topping is excellent on juicy fruits like peaches, berries or a combination. Use a shallow 12-cup (3 L) baking dish and 8 cups (2 L) prepared fruit.

*½ cup (125 mL) granulated sugar*

*½ tsp (2 mL) ground cinnamon*

*1½ cups (375 mL) all-purpose flour*

*1 tsp (5 mL) baking soda*

*Pinch salt*

*½ cup (125 mL) cold butter, cubed*

*2 eggs*

*1 cup (250 mL) buttermilk (page 171)*

*1 tsp (5 mL) vanilla*

In small bowl, combine 1 tbsp (15 mL) sugar with cinnamon.

In large bowl, combine remaining sugar, flour, baking soda and salt. Using hand pastry blender or 2 knives, cut in butter until texture resembles coarse crumbs.

In separate bowl, whisk together eggs, buttermilk and vanilla. Stir into dry mixture just until blended.

Drop batter by large spoonfuls over prepared fruit. Spread lightly but don't worry about covering fruit entirely, as topping will spread while baking. Sprinkle with cinnamon mixture.

Bake in preheated 375 F (190 C) oven about 35 minutes, or until topping is deep golden and fruit is bubbling up at edges.

*Makes 6 servings.*

◆ Sweeten fruit fillings to taste with granulated or brown sugar, honey or maple syrup. If pears or apples are sweet, I often don't add any sugar to the fruit, as the topping has lots. Rhubarb tends to need extra sugar – about ¾ cup (175 mL) for 6 cups (1.5 L) rhubarb.

◆ Bake crisps in a 350 F (180 C) oven about 45 minutes, or until fruit is tender and topping is crisp.

◆ If you are using frozen fruit, do not thaw before preparing, but bake 15 to 20 minutes longer.

◆ Some people like to press a little topping into the bottom of the pan. Although this is not traditional, it makes a bit of a crust.

# POACHED PEARS

2 lemons

2 cups (500 mL) water

2 cups (500 mL) dry white wine

1½ cups (375 mL) granulated sugar

2 tbsp (25 mL) vanilla

1 cinnamon stick

4 whole cloves

6 ripe pears or apples

*A* tried-and-true dessert that's at its best served with crisp cookies and chocolate sauce, raspberry sauce (page 123), thin custard or vanilla ice cream. Anjou pears or apples like Golden Delicious, Mutsu or Ida Red work well. Be sure to choose unblemished, firm but ripe fruit. An off-dry white wine would be good in this.

These could be oven-poached instead of cooked on top of the stove. Just pour the syrup over the peeled pears in a casserole or baking dish. Cook, covered, in a preheated 325 F (160 C) oven for about 30 minutes. If desired, add an orange to the lemons for a delicate flavour boost.

Using paring knife, peel yellow rind in strips from lemons. Squeeze lemons.

In large saucepan, combine lemon juice and rind with water, wine, sugar, vanilla, cinnamon stick and cloves. Bring to a boil and simmer about 5 minutes or until sugar has dissolved to form a syrup. Remove from heat.

Peel pears carefully to preserve shape and core. (Fruit can also be halved and cored. For an attractive presentation, try leaving stem on and removing core from bottom.) As each pear is peeled, drop into syrup to prevent browning. Bring to just below simmering, cover and cook about 15 minutes or until just tender when pierced with a knife. (If allowed to boil, fruit will split.) Turn fruit occasionally during cooking.

Cool in liquid at least 30 minutes before serving. If making ahead, leave in poaching liquid until ready to serve.

*Makes 6 servings.*

## Chocolate Sauce

A lower-fat chocolate sauce that's loaded with flavour, this would also be great with sundaes, pound cake or fruit compote.

In small saucepan, combine 1 cup (250 mL) cocoa powder with ¾ cup (175 mL) granulated sugar. Stir in ¾ cup (175 mL) water and ½ cup (125 mL) corn syrup. Place over medium heat and bring to a boil. Boil 2 full minutes, stirring constantly. Remove from heat, stir in 1 tsp (5 mL) vanilla and let cool completely. Sauce will thicken as it cools.

*Makes 2 cups (500 mL).*

# Ruth's Linzertorte

*1¼ cups (300 mL) whole unblanched almonds, skins on (6 oz/175 g)*

*¾ cup (175 mL) butter, at room temperature*

*½ cup (125 mL) granulated sugar*

*2 egg yolks, (reserve 1 white)*

*1 tsp (5 mL) finely grated lemon rind*

*1 tbsp (15 mL) lemon juice*

*1 cup (250 mL) all-purpose flour*

*1 tbsp (15 mL) cocoa powder*

*½ tsp (2 mL) ground cinnamon*

*Pinch ground cloves*

*About 1 cup (250 mL) good-quality raspberry jam*

*Icing sugar*

In food processor, finely chop almonds, pulsing with on/off motion just until ground.

In large bowl, using electric mixer, cream butter and sugar until fluffy. Add egg yolks, lemon rind and lemon juice. Beat until smooth.

In separate bowl, combine flour, cocoa, cinnamon, cloves and chopped almonds. Stir into butter mixture to form a soft dough. Gather dough into ball, wrap well in plastic wrap and refrigerate at least 1 hour or overnight. (If chilling overnight, allow to soften at room temperature 30 minutes before using.)

With floured hands, evenly pat two-thirds of dough onto bottom and about 1¼ inches (3 cm) up sides of 9-inch (23 cm) springform pan or fluted flan ring with removable bottom. Carefully spread jam over dough.

On floured surface, roll remaining dough into oval ¼ inch (.5 cm) thick. Cut into strips ¾ inch (2 cm) wide and arrange in lattice on top of jam, pressing edges into edge of torte. (If strips break, simply press them back together.)

Lightly beat reserved egg white. Brush strips and edges of torte with egg white.

Bake in preheated 350 F (180 C) oven about 45 minutes or until pastry is well browned and jam is bubbling. Cool completely in pan on rack. Remove sides. Dust with sifted icing sugar before serving with vanilla ice cream or crème fraîche (page 149).

*Makes 10 servings.*

When I turned twenty-one, my mother, Ruth Schachter (an ace baker whose European-style cakes and tortes are second to none), gave me the most precious present: a small folder filled with her favourite recipes. In it there were three versions of Linzertorte, a crunchy, toothsome dessert that originated in Austria. I took the one she rated tops and perfected it to come up with this superbly elegant dessert. Savour it with a cup of tea or coffee or to round off a fine homecooked meal. This is a shallow, rich, nut-crusted tart with a jam filling. The dough is delicate, which means making the lattice topping can be tricky. Don't bother trying to weave it; just do it criss-cross style. This dough makes great thumbprint cookies filled with jam.

# Plum Tart

*Plums are one of my favourite fruits to use in baking. They have luscious texture and loads of flavour. This tart has a smooth custard layer – delish! You could also use fresh peaches when they are in season. The Plum Kuchen made with a sweetened pastry is another dessert from my mother.*

| |
|---|
| *1½ cups (375 mL) all-purpose flour* |
| *¼ cup (50 mL) granulated sugar* |
| *½ tsp (2 mL) salt* |
| *¼ tsp (1 mL) baking powder* |
| *1 tbsp (15 mL) finely grated orange rind* |
| *¼ cup (50 mL) cold butter, cubed* |
| *¼ cup (50 mL) cold shortening, cubed* |
| *1 egg* |
| *1 tsp (5 mL) water* |
| *1 lb (500 g) small purple plums (about 12), halved and pitted* |

## Topping:

| |
|---|
| *3 tbsp (45 mL) granulated sugar* |
| *2 tsp (10 mL) all-purpose flour* |
| *⅓ cup (75 mL) light cream (10 percent or 18 percent)* |
| *1 tbsp (15 mL) Grand Marnier or other orange liqueur (optional)* |
| *1 egg* |
| *½ tsp (2 mL) vanilla* |

In bowl, combine flour, sugar, salt and baking powder. Using fork, toss in orange rind until evenly distributed.

Using hand pastry blender or 2 knives, cut in butter and shortening until texture of coarse crumbs.

In small bowl, beat egg with water. Stir into pastry just until dough begins to clump. Work dough gently with hands to form a smooth ball. Wrap in plastic wrap and refrigerate 30 minutes. Press dough evenly into 10-inch (25 cm) flan pan.

Arrange plums, skin side up, on top of pastry. Bake in preheated 375 F (190 C) oven 30 minutes.

Meanwhile, to prepare topping, in small bowl, combine sugar and flour. Whisk in cream, Grand Marnier (if using), egg and vanilla. Pour over plums. Bake 15 minutes or until custard is puffed and golden. Cool completely before serving.

*Makes 8 servings.*

## Peach Pie

From the Fedorkow family who, at Fruithaven Farms, grow peaches in Ontario's lush Niagara region. Adjust the amount of sugar in the topping to taste and cool the pie to room temperature before serving so the peaches aren't too runny.

Peel 5 large, ripe peaches (page 146) and place in 9-inch (23 cm) unbaked pie shell.

In bowl, combine ½ cup (125 mL) granulated sugar, 2 tbsp (25 mL) all-purpose flour and 1 tsp (5 mL) ground cinnamon. With hand pastry blender, cut in 2 tbsp (25 mL) cold butter until mixture resembles coarse crumbs. Spoon mixture evenly over peaches.

In bowl, combine 2 well-beaten eggs, 1 tsp (5 mL) vanilla and a pinch of salt. Pour over pie. Bake pie in preheated 400 F (200 C) oven 15 minutes. Reduce heat to 325 F (160 C) and bake about 40 minutes or until set and browned.

*Makes 6 servings.*

## Sweet Pastry

In bowl, combine 1 cup (250 mL) all-purpose flour, 1 tbsp (15 mL) granulated sugar and a pinch of salt. Using hand pastry blender, cut in ½ cup (125 mL) cold butter, cubed, until mixture resembles coarse crumbs. Stir in 1 beaten egg yolk just until mixture begins to clump. Form dough gently into ball and press into bottom of lightly greased 8 or 9-inch (20 or 23 cm) round baking pan.

## Plum Kuchen

Top unbaked 8 or 9-inch (20 or 23 cm) unbaked sweet pastry shell (above) with 1 cup (250 mL) cake crumbs (crumbled soft ladyfingers or leftover pound cake work well). Sprinkle with pinch ground cinnamon. Pit and quarter about 6 small purple plums (8 oz/250 g). Arrange in concentric circles, skin side up, to cover pastry. Sprinkle with 2 tbsp (25 mL) slivered almonds and 1 tsp (5 mL) granulated sugar.

Bake in preheated 400 F (200 C) oven about 30 minutes or until plums are tender and pastry is golden. Sprinkle with a little sifted icing sugar. Serve as is or with sweetened plain yogurt, vanilla ice cream or crème fraîche (page 149).

*Makes 6 servings.*

# PEACHY KEEN PAVLOVA

## YOGURT CREAM:

*3 cups (750 mL) plain yogurt*

*2 tbsp (25 mL) granulated sugar*

*Finely grated rind of 1 lemon*

## MERINGUE:

*4 egg whites, at room temperature*

*¼ tsp (1 mL) salt*

*1 cup (250 mL) granulated sugar*

*2 tsp (10 mL) lemon juice or white vinegar*

*2 tsp (10 mL) cornstarch*

*1 tsp (5 mL) vanilla*

## FILLING:

*4 fresh peaches*

*1 tbsp (15 mL) granulated sugar*

*1 tbsp (15 mL) lemon juice*

*1 tbsp (15 mL) peach schnapps, Amaretto or orange liqueur (optional)*

To prepare yogurt cream, in bowl, combine yogurt, sugar and lemon rind. Place in sieve lined with cheesecloth or a clean tea towel. Place sieve over a bowl and refrigerate overnight. Discard liquid in bowl or use in bread or muffin recipes.

To prepare meringue, using electric mixer, beat egg whites and salt until soft peaks form. Gradually beat in sugar, one tablespoon at a time, until meringue is stiff and glossy.

In small bowl, stir together lemon juice, cornstarch and vanilla. Fold into meringue.

On baking sheet lined with parchment or waxed paper, trace a 10-inch (25 cm) circle. Spread meringue inside this circle, swirling up sides to make a nest.

Bake in preheated 250 F (120 C) oven 2 hours or until firm at edges but slightly soft in centre and lightly golden. Turn off oven. Let meringue cool completely in oven at least 2 hours but preferably overnight.

To prepare filling, peel peaches by plunging them into boiling water 30 to 60 seconds. Transfer to bowl of cold water with slotted spoon. Slip skins off. Pit and slice peaches.

*T*his elegant meringue dessert created by Foodland Ontario is based on the famous Australian creation named after the Russian ballerina Anna Pavlova. Peaches are ideal, but strawberries, blueberries, kiwi or mango would also work well. All the components of this dish can be made ahead (the meringue and yogurt cream are, in fact, best made in advance) but it must be assembled just before serving or the meringue will become mushy. (Making this on a humid summer's day will also result in a soft meringue.) The yogurt cream is a great low-fat alternative to whipped cream; it can be used as a garnish or ingredient in other desserts.

In large bowl, toss peaches with sugar, lemon juice and liqueur (if using).

To serve, carefully peel paper from meringue. Place meringue on serving plate. Spoon yogurt cream into centre of meringue "nest." Top with peaches and serve immediately.

*Makes 8 servings.*

# RHUBARB COMPOTE

| |
|---|
| *3 cups (750 mL) apple juice or white wine* |
| *6 stalks fresh rhubarb, cut in 1-inch (2.5 cm) pieces* |
| *¼ cup (50 mL) liquid honey* |
| *2 tbsp (25 mL) finely chopped crystallized ginger (optional)* |
| *Finely grated rind and juice of 1 lemon* |
| *½ cup (125 mL) water* |
| *½ cup (125 mL) raisins* |
| *10 prunes, pitted and chopped* |
| *½ cup (125 mL) chopped dates* |
| *½ cup (125 mL) dried apricots, thinly sliced* |
| *½ cup (125 mL) dried cherries or cranberries* |

In saucepan, combine apple juice, rhubarb, honey, ginger (if using), lemon rind and juice and water. Bring to a boil, reduce heat to low, cover and simmer about 10 minutes. Add raisins, prunes, dates, apricots and cherries. Bring to simmer, cover and cook 15 minutes. Serve warm or at room temperature.

*Makes 6 servings.*

*T*art, fresh rhubarb and sweet dried fruit combine here to produce one of the best desserts I've tasted. The idea comes from a cookbook called *Recipes from Riversong* by terrific cook Pat Crocker, who gives workshops and leads herb walks at her lovely 150-year-old log cabin near Mount Forest north of Metro. Fabulous with vanilla ice cream, sweetened plain yogurt or crème fraîche (page 149), the compote could also be spooned over pound cake or even eaten with pancakes or cereal for a breakfast dish. This keeps in the fridge for up to three weeks and freezes well.

# MARION'S APPLE PIE

| |
|---|
| 2 cups (500 mL) all-purpose flour |
| ½ cup (125 mL) cold butter, cubed |
| ¼ cup (50 mL) cold vegetable shortening, cubed |
| ¼ cup (50 mL) cold lard, cubed |
| ½ cup (125 mL) ice-cold water |
| 1 egg |
| 5 to 6 large tart apples, peeled, cored and sliced |
| 2 tbsp (25 mL) brown or granulated sugar |
| 2 tbsp (25 mL) lemon juice |
| ½ tsp (2 mL) ground cinnamon |
| 2 tbsp (25 mL) milk |

*O*ne of my several careers before I became a food editor was as a freelance pie-maker selling my apple pies to local restaurants. This metier was hard work and not too lucrative but it did enable me to perfect this dessert, which I began making with my mother's tutelage. Using three types of fat for the pastry gives amazing taste and texture, although you could use just one or two types with almost as good results. The other trick is to keep your hands and head cool when handling the dough. I advocate the old-fashioned manual wire pastry blender for cutting the fat into the flour. I also like the food processor. Pulse all ingredients except water in food processor 5 or 6 times until mixture resembles coarse crumbs. Pulsing, add water gradually through feeder tube. Gather dough into a ball and proceed as in this recipe. Use any tart, firm apple for the filling. However, the pie is truly superb when made in the fall with freshly picked Northern Spys, by far the best pie-making apples grown in these parts. You could substitute plums or pears for some of the apples. Serve with sweetened plain yogurt, vanilla ice cream, crème fraîche (page 149) or whipped cream.

For pastry, place flour in large bowl. Using wire hand pastry blender, cut in butter, shortening and lard until mixture resembles coarse crumbs. Sprinkle with ice water. Toss with fork and quickly gather dough into ball. Wrap in plastic wrap and chill about 30 minutes.

Divide dough into two balls, one slightly bigger than the other. Shape each ball into flat disc with floured hands. On lightly floured surface, roll larger disc to fit 9-inch (23 cm) pie plate including 1-inch (2.5 cm) overhanging edge. Place pastry over pie plate and gently pat in place.

Separate egg, placing white and yolk in separate small bowls. Brush lightly beaten egg white over pastry in pie plate to keep it crisp during baking.

In large bowl, toss together apples, sugar, lemon juice and cinnamon.

Arrange mixture in pie plate, shaking gently to settle apples.

Roll out remaining dough to fit top of pie, including slight overhang.

Whisk together egg yolk and milk for egg wash. Brush around rim of pie. Place rolled dough over apples. Tuck edges under, cutting off any excess, and flute edges using thumb of one hand to press dough down and forefinger of other hand to pull dough up. Make leaves or flowers from excess dough to decorate centre of pie, if desired. Prick top of pie with fork at least a dozen times to let steam escape. Brush pastry evenly with egg wash.

Bake in preheated 350F (180C) oven 50 minutes or until crust is golden-brown.

*Makes 6 to 8 servings.*

# CRÈME FRAÎCHE

## CLASSIC CRÈME FRAÎCHE

In bowl, combine 1 cup (250 mL) whipping cream with 1 cup (250 mL) sour cream or plain yogurt. Cover and let stand at room temperature 24 hours or until thickened. Refrigerate until using.

*Makes about 2 cups (500 mL).*

## SWEETENED CRÈME FRAÎCHE

In bowl, combine 1½ cups (375 mL) whipping cream, ¼ cup (50 mL) plain yogurt, ¼ cup (50 mL) granulated sugar, 2 tbsp (25 mL) lemon juice and ¼ tsp (1 mL) vanilla. Cover and let stand at room temperature about 24 hours or until thickened. Refrigerate until using.

*Makes about 2 cups (500 mL).*

## LOW-FAT CRÈME FRAÎCHE

In bowl, combine 1 cup (250 mL) low-fat plain yogurt, 1 cup (250 mL) low-fat sour cream, ¼ cup (50 mL) granulated sugar and ½ tsp (2 mL) vanilla. Use immediately or refrigerate until serving time.

*Makes about 2 cups (500 mL).*

# APPLESAUCE

*6 apples, cored and sliced*

*Juice of half a lemon (2 tbsp/25 mL)*

*2 tbsp (25 mL) granulated sugar*
*or 1 tbsp (15 mL) liquid honey*

*½ tsp (2 mL) ground cinnamon*

In ovenproof dish or casserole with lid (I use an earthenware dish covered tightly with foil), combine apples, lemon juice, sugar and cinnamon.

Bake, covered, in 350 F (180 C) oven about 1 hour or until fruit is soft and bubbly. Purée in food processor until smooth.

*Makes 3 cups (750 mL).*

*A* wondrous accompaniment to serve with fruit compotes, pies and other sweets, or even, in an unsweetened version, with vegetables such as steamed asparagus. The low-fat version could easily become savoury by omitting the sugar and vanilla.

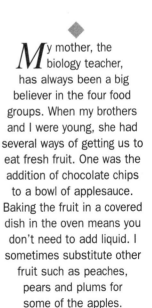

*M* y mother, the biology teacher, has always been a big believer in the four food groups. When my brothers and I were young, she had several ways of getting us to eat fresh fruit. One was the addition of chocolate chips to a bowl of applesauce. Baking the fruit in a covered dish in the oven means you don't need to add liquid. I sometimes substitute other fruit such as peaches, pears and plums for some of the apples.

# CHOCOLATE TRUFFLES

*I* learned about these delectable morsels from talented caterer Dawn Adrienne Berney, when I wrote about the annual fundraiser for Second Harvest – a non-profit group that redistributes leftover perishable food to shelters and hostels around Metro. She made and served them at the glitzy gala event along with the fabulous wares of many of Toronto's top chefs.

President's Choice bittersweet chocolate works well although, of course, Lindt and the harder-to-find Callebaut chocolate would also be excellent. A terrific hostess gift, after-dinner sweet or holiday munchie.

*8 oz (250 g) bittersweet chocolate*
*1 cup (250 mL) unsalted butter*
*½ cup (125 mL) whipping cream*
*10 oz (300 g) semisweet chocolate*
*1 cup (250 mL) cocoa powder, sifted*

In top of double boiler over barely simmering water, melt bittersweet chocolate and butter. Cool to room temperature.

Meanwhile, in bowl, whip cream to soft peaks. Fold into chocolate mixture. Refrigerate 15 minutes to harden slightly.

Line baking sheet with foil. Using melon baller, scoop out a spoonful of chocolate mixture and place on baking sheet. Repeat using remaining mixture. Refrigerate balls 15 minutes.

Melt semisweet chocolate in top of double boiler over barely simmering water. Cool to room temperature.

Place cocoa in shallow dish. Dip each chocolate ball into melted chocolate, turning to coat evenly and letting excess chocolate drip off. Place in cocoa and shake dish to coat. Store in airtight container, refrigerated, until ready to serve. Dust with cocoa again before serving.

*Makes about 45 truffles.*

# *Home for the Holidays*

# TOURTIÈRE

A wonderful version of a fabulous Québécois Christmas and New Year's Eve tradition, this comes from Melanie Simpson, owner of Toronto restaurant, Montreal's Deli and Wine Bar. Serve this deftly spiced meat pie with your favourite chutney (green tomato relish is delectable with it) or other condiment. The pastry, made with hot water by an unconventional method, is so good you'll want to use it for other pies.

## PASTRY:

1 cup (250 mL) vegetable shortening or lard, at room temperature

½ cup (125 mL) boiling water

2½ cups (625 mL) all-purpose flour

1 tsp (5 mL) baking powder

¼ tsp (1 mL) salt

## FILLING:

1 potato, peeled

1 lb (500 g) ground pork

1 onion, finely chopped

1 stalk celery, cut in 3 pieces

1 clove garlic, finely chopped

¾ tsp (4 mL) salt

½ tsp (2 mL) dried thyme

¾ tsp (4 mL) ground sage

¼ tsp (1 mL) ground cloves

Freshly ground black pepper to taste

1 egg

1 tbsp (15 mL) water

To make pastry, place shortening in food processor. Pour in boiling water. Process, pulsing, until combined. In bowl, combine flour, baking powder and salt. Gradually add to shortening mixture in food processor; pulse, scraping down sides as necessary, to form smooth, soft dough. Wrap in plastic wrap and refrigerate while making filling.

For filling, cut potato into large chunks. Place in saucepan, cover with water and bring to a boil. Boil 15 minutes or until soft. Drain, reserving ½ cup (125 mL) cooking water.

In saucepan, combine reserved potato water, pork, onion, celery, garlic, salt, thyme, sage and cloves. Bring to a boil, reduce heat and simmer, uncovered, about 30 minutes or until vegetables are tender, pork is no longer pink and water has evaporated. Discard celery. Season with pepper.

Meanwhile, in bowl, mash potato with fork. Stir into meat mixture and cool completely.

On lightly floured surface, roll out half of dough until about

⅛ inch (.25 cm) thick. Place in 9-inch (23 cm) pie plate and fill with meat mixture. Roll out remaining dough and place over filling. Trim and flute edges. (Use any leftover dough, if desired, to make attractive leaves or other shapes and place on top of unbaked pie.)

In small bowl, beat egg with water. Brush over pastry. Cut steam vents in top.

Bake pie in preheated 450 F (230 C) oven 10 minutes. Reduce heat to 350 F (180 C) and bake 25 minutes longer or until pastry is golden.

*Makes 6 servings.*

# POTATO LATKES

*3 cups (750 mL) unpeeled, cubed raw potatoes (3 medium)*

*1 large onion, quartered*

*3 eggs*

*2 tbsp (25 mL) all-purpose flour*

*1 tsp (5 mL) baking powder*

*½ tsp (2 mL) salt*

*¼ tsp (1 mL) freshly ground black pepper*

*Vegetable oil for frying*

In food processor, in batches if necessary, combine potatoes, onion, eggs, flour, baking powder, salt and pepper, pulsing with on/off motion just until coarsely chopped. Do not overprocess; mixture should be shredded, not mushy.

Add oil to large skillet until ½ inch (1 cm) deep and heat over medium heat.

Spoon potato mixture into oil – about 3 tbsp (45 mL) per pancake. Cook about 4 minutes, turn and cook about 5 minutes or until golden and crisp on both sides. Drain on paper towels. Repeat with remaining batter.

*Makes about 16 pancakes.*

An absolute must for Jewish Chanukah celebrations, these are pretty classic and pretty darned good. Instead of frying the latkes the traditional way, you could reduce the fat by cooking them in a non-stick pan that has been lightly brushed with oil. You could also add an extra egg white to the potato mixture, form it into patties, place them on a greased baking sheet and bake the latkes in a preheated 450 F (230 C) oven for about 15 minutes, turning them once. You can grate the potatoes and onion by hand (considered *de rigueur* by some cooks), but I find that the food processor works perfectly well. As usual, I like to use Yukon Gold potatoes, but your basic spuds would be fine.

# Vegetarian "Turkey"

*Visit the market to purchase a large, attractive squash to make a stylish presentation for this incredible meatless substitute for the holiday turkey. Inspired by a recipe from CBC radio host Vicki Gabereau's Cooking Without Looking, our creation will be a hit with meat-eaters and vegetarians alike. It makes an elegant, delicious centrepiece for any festive feast.*

*5-lb (2.5 kg) whole winter squash (e.g., buttercup or pumpkin)*

*½ cup (125 mL) dried brown lentils*

*1 onion, chopped*

*1 bay leaf*

*½ cup (125 mL) raw brown rice*

*½ cup (125 mL) raw millet*

*1 tbsp (15 mL) vegetable oil*

*1 clove garlic, finely chopped*

*1 large stalk celery, chopped*

*2 cups (500 mL) broccoli florets (6 oz/175 g)*

*1 tbsp (15 mL) soy sauce*

*1 tbsp (15 mL) chopped fresh sage, or 1 tsp (5 mL) dried*

*1 tsp (5 mL) celery seed*

*1 tsp (5 mL) chopped fresh thyme, or ¼ tsp (1 mL) dried*

*½ tsp (2 mL) salt*

*¼ tsp (1 mL) freshly ground black pepper*

*½ cup (125 mL) almonds or cashews, chopped*

*2 tbsp (25 mL) unsalted sunflower seeds (optional)*

## Meatless Gravy:

*¼ cup (50 mL) vegetable oil*

*1 small onion, finely chopped*

*1 clove garlic, finely chopped*

*1 tbsp (15 mL) chopped fresh rosemary, or 1 tsp (5 mL) dried*

*¼ cup (50 mL) all-purpose flour*

*3 cups (750 mL) vegetable stock*

*Salt and freshly ground black pepper to taste*

In preheated 300 F (150 C) oven, bake whole squash 1 hour. Cool slightly. Cut circle in top and remove "lid." With spoon, scoop out seeds and pulp.

Meanwhile, in saucepan, combine lentils, ¼ cup (50 mL) chopped onion and bay leaf. Cover with 2 cups (500 mL) water. Bring to a boil, reduce heat and simmer, covered, 1 hour. Discard bay leaf.

In separate saucepan, combine rice with 1 cup (250 mL)

water.  Bring to a boil, reduce heat and simmer, covered, 45 minutes.

In another saucepan, cover millet with 1 cup (250 mL) water. Bring to a boil, reduce heat and simmer, covered, 20 minutes or until water is absorbed.

Heat oil in large skillet over medium heat. Add remaining onion, garlic and celery.  Cook about 4 minutes or until softened. Stir in lentils, with any remaining liquid, broccoli, soy sauce, sage, celery seed, thyme, salt and pepper.  Bring just to a boil. Add rice, millet, almonds and sunflower seeds (if using), stirring just until combined. Taste stuffing and adjust seasoning.

Stuff squash with as much stuffing as possible. If any remains, place in greased loaf pan and bake, covered, along with squash.

Place "lid" back on squash.  Set squash upright in roasting pan. Bake in preheated 350 F (180 C) oven 1 hour or until squash is tender when tested with a fork.

Meanwhile, to prepare gravy, heat oil in saucepan over medium heat. Stir in onion, garlic and rosemary.  Cook 5 minutes or until softened but not browned.

Add flour, stirring to make a paste. Gradually whisk in vegetable stock until smooth. Increase heat, bring to a boil, and cook, stirring, about 3 minutes or until thickened. Add salt and pepper.

To serve, slice filled squash in wedges and pass gravy on the side.

*Makes 8 to 10 servings.*

# OLD-FASHIONED STUFFING

This is an old-fashioned bread stuffing with a couple of new twists, namely the dried fruit soaked in liqueur. The fruit and pecans are optional, but if you don't use them, increase the amount of bread to 14 cups (3.5 L). I sometimes toast the bread cubes before incorporating them into the stuffing by spreading them on a greased baking sheet in a single layer and baking in a 400 F (200 C) oven for about 10 minutes or until golden. I also sometimes put some of the stuffing in the neck cavity and between the skin and breast meat for a tasty change.

| |
|---|
| 1 cup (250 mL) raisins, chopped dried apricots or chopped prunes, or a mixture (optional) |
| ½ cup (125 mL) orange liqueur, Port, sherry or fruit juice (optional) |
| ½ cup (125 mL) butter |
| 4 large stalks celery, chopped |
| 2 large onions, chopped |
| 1 large apple, unpeeled, cored and diced |
| 1 tbsp (15 mL) dried sage |
| 1 tsp (5 mL) dried thyme |
| 1 tsp (5 mL) dried savory |
| ¾ tsp (3 mL) salt |
| ¼ tsp (1 mL) freshly ground black pepper |
| 12 cups (3 L) ½-inch (1 cm) bread cubes |
| 1 cup (250 mL) coarsely chopped pecans (optional) |
| ¾ cup (175 mL) chicken stock |

In small saucepan, combine raisins and liqueur (if using). Bring to a boil and set aside.

Melt butter in very large skillet or saucepan over medium heat. Add celery, onions and apple. Cook, stirring occasionally, about 6 minutes or until onion is softened. Stir in sage, thyme, savory, salt and pepper. Cook about 1 minute or until fragrant. Add bread cubes and pecans (if using), stirring to coat with seasonings. Add fruit mixture (if using) and stock, stirring to moisten.

Stuff into cavity of turkey just before roasting.

*Makes enough for a 16- to 18-lb (5.75 to 6 kg) turkey.*

# TURKEY GRAVY

*Turkey drippings*

*1 small onion, chopped*

*¼ cup (50 mL) all-purpose flour*

*¼ cup (50 mL) dry white wine (optional)*

*3 cups (750 mL) turkey, chicken or vegetable stock*

*Salt and freshly ground black pepper to taste*

Pour drippings from roasting pan into large measuring cup. Allow fat to rise to the top. Return about ¼ cup (50 mL) fat to pan. Discard remaining fat, but reserve any other drippings.

Place roasting pan over medium heat. Add onion and cook, stirring, about 4 minutes or until onion is softened. Whisk in flour and cook, stirring constantly, 1 minute. Pour in wine (if using), stock and remaining drippings. Bring to a boil and reduce heat. Whisk over low heat, scraping up brown bits from bottom of pan, until smooth and thickened. Add salt and pepper. Pour gravy through a sieve, if desired.

*Makes about 3 cups (750 mL).*

The gravy is surely a crucial ingredient at Thanksgiving and Christmas or any time, in fact, when you're serving roast turkey. I always make stock for it by simmering the bird's giblets (minus the liver – it adds an unpleasant taste) while the turkey is roasting. Cover the giblets with cold water in a saucepan. Add a sliced carrot and a clove of garlic. Bring to a boil and simmer, uncovered, about 1 hour.

## TALKING TURKEY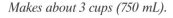

**Turkey times:** For roasting whole stuffed turkeys, in preheated 325F (160C) oven:

| Kg | Min/kg | Hours |
|---|---|---|
| 3 to 3.5 | 60 | 3 to 3¼ |
| 3.5 to 4.5 | 50 | 3¼ to 3½ |
| 4.5 to 5.5 | 45 | 3½ to 3¾ |
| 5.5 to 7 | 40 | 3¾ to 4 |
| 7 to 10 | 30 | 4 to 4½ |

For unstuffed turkey, reduce cooking time by 10 minutes per kilogram.  1 kg = 2.2 lb.

■ Remove neck and giblets from bird's cavity; rinse turkey inside and out.
■ Stuff bird just before roasting. Fold neck skin over and skewer it to back. Twist wings under back. Tuck legs under band of skin or tie together with string.
■ Place turkey on rack in roasting pan breast side up. Brush with vegetable oil before roasting; season as desired.
■ Tent with foil, leaving sides open. Roast in 325F (160C) oven. Refer to chart as a guideline.
■ Insert thermometer into inner thigh, just above but not touching thigh bone. When done, it should read 180F (82C) for a stuffed turkey, 170F (77C) for an unstuffed turkey. Remove foil for last half hour to allow turkey to brown. Place on cutting board or platter, cover with foil and let stand 15 to 20 minutes before carving.

# CRANBERRY CHESTNUT SALAD

*1½ cups (375 mL) cranberries, coarsely chopped*

*3 tbsp (45 mL) granulated sugar*

*12 oz (375 g) fresh chestnuts (about 10)*

*3 tbsp (45 mL) lemon juice*

*2 tsp (10 mL) Dijon mustard*

*¼ tsp (1 mL) salt*

*⅓ cup (75 mL) olive oil*

*3 tart apples, cored and cut in chunks*

*3 green onions, chopped*

*2 bunches watercress, tough stems removed*

In bowl, combine cranberries and sugar. Let stand in refrigerator 1 hour or overnight.

To peel chestnuts, cut shallow X on round side with small sharp knife. Place on baking sheet. Roast chestnuts in preheated 375 F (190 C) oven about 20 minutes or until edges of X have peeled back from flesh. (Or, place chestnuts in large saucepan of cold water. Bring to a boil, reduce heat and simmer, covered, 20 minutes. Drain.)  Let chestnuts cool slightly. Peel off shells and brown skin while still warm (flesh may be crumbly). Quarter any whole chestnut pieces.

In large bowl, whisk together lemon juice, mustard, salt and oil until smooth. Stir in chestnuts, apples and green onions. Let stand at least 1 hour or up to 4 hours, refrigerated.

To serve, line platter or large bowl with watercress. Place apple mixture around edges and pile cranberries in centre.

*Makes 8 servings.*

---

*I* learned to make this gorgeous salad from my long-time friend Frances Beaulieu, author of the popular *Toronto Star* recipe cartoon, Recipix. Fresh cranberries are best, but thawed frozen berries will do. Whichever type you use, they can be chopped in the food processor, if desired. This salad looks as luscious as it tastes and is a refreshing addition to a Thanksgiving or Christmas feast. Be careful to remove all the tough stems from the watercress. Although it's not absolutely necessary since the lemon in the dressing will prevent discolouration in the apples, Cortland apples have the amazing quality of not oxidizing (turning brown) when sliced and are therefore ideal for salads or fruit plates.

---

# FRESH CRANBERRY RELISH

*1 orange, unpeeled, washed, quartered and seeded*

*2 cups (500 mL) fresh cranberries*

*½ cup (125 mL) granulated sugar*

In food processor, coarsely chop orange and cranberries. Place in glass or ceramic bowl. Stir in sugar. Refrigerate at least 1 day or up to 4 days before serving.

*Makes about 2 cups (500 mL).*

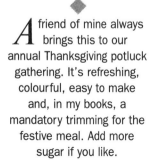

*A* friend of mine always brings this to our annual Thanksgiving potluck gathering. It's refreshing, colourful, easy to make and, in my books, a mandatory trimming for the festive meal. Add more sugar if you like.

# LIGHTER PUMPKIN PIE

## LOW-FAT PASTRY:

| | |
|---|---|
| 1½ cups (375 mL) all-purpose flour | |
| ½ tsp (2 mL) salt | |
| 2 tbsp (25 mL) cold butter, cubed | |
| ¼ cup (50 mL) vegetable oil | |
| 1 tbsp (15 mL) white vinegar | |
| 3 tbsp (45 mL) ice-cold water | |

## FILLING:

| | |
|---|---|
| 14-oz (398 mL) can pumpkin purée (1¾ cups/425 mL) | |
| 1 cup (250 mL) brown sugar | |
| 1 egg | |
| 2 egg whites | |
| 1¼ cups (300 mL) low-fat evaporated milk | |
| 1 tsp (5 mL) vanilla | |
| 1 tsp (5 mL) ground cinnamon | |
| ½ tsp (2 mL) ground ginger | |
| ¼ tsp (1 mL) ground allspice | |
| ¼ tsp (1 mL) grated nutmeg | |
| Pinch salt | |

*This low-fat crust – crisp, flaky and loaded with flavour – would work on any pie. It has slightly less fat and a lot less saturated fat than most pie crusts. I also reduced the fat in the pumpkin filling by using low-fat milk and only one whole egg. For another lower-fat pastry, try the Pat-in Pastry (page 161) from Edna Staebler, author of More Food That Really Schmecks and Schmecks Appeal in which that recipe appears.*

For pastry, combine flour and salt in bowl. Using wire hand pastry blender, cut in butter until texture of crumbs. Sprinkle oil over flour and toss with fork until blended.

In small bowl or cup, combine vinegar and water. Sprinkle over flour and toss with fork until dough begins to form a ball.

Gather dough into soft ball. Between two sheets of waxed paper or plastic wrap, roll out dough to ⅛-inch (.25 cm) thickness. Place in 9-inch (23 cm) pie plate. Trim and flute edges; refrigerate shell about 15 minutes before baking.

Meanwhile, to prepare filling, in bowl, combine pumpkin purée, brown sugar, egg and egg whites, milk, vanilla, cinnamon, ginger, allspice, nutmeg and salt until smooth. Pour into chilled shell.

Bake in preheated 375 F (190 C) oven about 50 minutes, or until just set in centre.

*Makes 6 to 8 servings.*

# CLASSIC PUMPKIN PIE

| |
|---|
| *14-oz (398 mL) can pumpkin purée (1¾ cups/425 mL)* |
| *2 eggs* |
| *¾ cup (175 mL) milk* |
| *¾ cup (175 mL) maple syrup* |
| *1 tsp (5 mL)  ground cinnamon* |
| *½ tsp (2 mL) ground ginger* |
| *¼ tsp (1 mL) ground cloves* |
| *¼ tsp (1 mL) grated nutmeg* |
| *¼ tsp (1 mL) salt* |
| *9-inch (23 cm) unbaked pie shell* |

*A*n all-Canadian version made with maple syrup; you could substitute an equal quantity of brown sugar to reduce the cost. If so, increase the milk to 1 cup (250 mL). Instead of regular milk, canned evaporated – low-fat or otherwise – could be used for a rich flavour.  If you are adding a topping to the pie, make sure your pie pan is deep enough to hold the topping as well as the pumpkin filling. Try our sour cream or meringue topping as well as pastry and filling variations.

In bowl, whisk together pumpkin, eggs, milk, maple syrup, cinnamon, ginger, cloves, nutmeg and salt until smooth.  Pour into pie shell.

Bake in preheated 375 F (190 C) oven about 45 minutes or until almost set but slightly soft in centre. Cool completely before serving.

*Makes 6 servings.*

## SOUR CREAM TOPPING:

Pour this over your hot, baked pumpkin pie to form a tasty, white top layer. Or, to create a spiderweb effect, place sour cream mixture in small piping bag with round tip or in plastic ketchup or mustard squeeze bottle with narrow nozzle. On unbaked pumpkin filling, pipe a spiral, starting at outer edge and finishing at centre. Using tip of a small paring knife, draw a shallow "line" with sour cream mixture through filling from outer edge to centre.  Repeat at 7 evenly spaced intervals around pie. Between each "line"  draw 8 more lines, going from centre to outer edge. Bake pie as described above.

| |
|---|
| *¾ cup (175 mL) sour cream* |
| *2 tbsp (25 mL) granulated sugar* |

Combine sour cream and sugar.  Spread over hot baked pie leaving ½-inch (1 cm) border around edges uncovered.  Return pie to oven for about 7 minutes or until just set.

## MERINGUE:

Instead of whole eggs, use 3 egg yolks in pie filling, then use the whites for this topping to add height and elegance.

*3 egg whites*

*1 tsp (5 mL) lemon juice*

*½ cup (125 mL) granulated sugar*

*½ tsp (2 mL) vanilla*

In bowl, beat egg whites and lemon juice until frothy. Gradually add sugar 1 tbsp (15 mL) at a time, beating until stiff but not dry. Beat in vanilla.

Cover hot, baked pie with meringue, creating attractive peaks. Return to 375 F (190 C) oven for about 8 minutes or until topping is golden.

## *Edna Staebler's Pat-in Pastry*

In 9-inch (23 cm) pie plate, combine 1½ cups (375 mL) all-purpose flour, 1½ tsp (7 mL) granulated sugar and ¾ tsp (4 mL) salt.

In small bowl, combine ½ cup (125 mL) vegetable oil (canola works well) and 3 tbsp (45 mL) cold milk, beating with fork until thick and creamy. Pour over flour mixture and mix with fork until flour mixture is completely moistened.

With fingers, pat dough over bottom and sides of pie plate, leaving enough dough to flute edges. Flute edges. Crust can be baked filled or unfilled.

*Makes one 9-inch (23 cm) single pie shell.*

## *Pumpkin Mincemeat Pie*

In large bowl, whisk together 14-oz (398 mL) can pumpkin purée (1¾ cups/425 mL), 2 eggs, ¾ cup (175 mL) light cream or evaporated milk, ½ cup (125 mL) brown sugar, ½ tsp (2 mL) each ground cinnamon and ground ginger, ¼ tsp (1 mL) each ground cloves and salt.

Spread 1 cup (250 mL) mincemeat in 9-inch (23 cm) unbaked deep-dish pie shell. Top with pumpkin mixture.

Bake in preheated 375 F (190 C) oven about 45 minutes, or until pumpkin is just set in centre.

*Makes 6 servings.*

# MOCK MINCEMEAT PIE

These days, many families include at least one vegetarian. I came up with a terrific meatless version of this Christmas standby using vegetables and fruit. If you are using homemade pastry, roll out the scraps and cut shapes with cookie cutters. Place the shapes decoratively on top of the filling before baking your pie.

The idea for this – mincemeat minus the meat product, beef suet – came from Foodland Ontario. Instead of making one large pie, you could use the mixture to make tarts or, by wrapping the mincemeat mixture in phyllo or puff pastry before baking, yummy little turnovers.

| |
|---|
| 2 tbsp (25 mL) butter |
| 1 large onion, finely chopped |
| 1 cup (250 mL) thinly sliced cabbage |
| 2 pears, peeled, cored and finely chopped |
| 2 apples, peeled, cored and finely chopped |
| 1 cup (250 mL) raisins |
| ½ cup (125 mL) currants |
| ½ cup (125 mL) apple juice |
| ½ cup (125 mL) brown sugar |
| Finely grated rind of 1 orange |
| Finely grated rind of 1 lemon |
| Juice of 2 oranges |
| Juice of 1 lemon |
| ¼ cup (50 mL) rum |
| ¼ cup (50 mL) chopped pecans (1 oz/30 g) |
| ¾ tsp (4 mL) ground cinnamon |
| ¼ tsp (1 mL) ground cloves |
| Unbaked 9-inch (23 cm) pie shell |

Melt butter in large saucepan over medium heat. Add onion and cabbage. Cook, stirring occasionally, about 7 minutes or until very soft. Stir in pears, apples, raisins, currants, apple juice, brown sugar, orange and lemon rind and juice, rum, pecans, cinnamon and cloves. Simmer about 20 minutes, stirring occasionally to prevent sticking, until fruit is tender and liquid has been absorbed. Cool completely.

Pour mixture into pie shell. Bake in preheated 425 F (220 C) oven about 35 minutes or until pastry is golden and filling is bubbling.

*Makes 6 servings.*

# DARK FRUITCAKE

*1½ cups (375 mL) raisins (8 oz/250 g)*

*1½ cups (375 mL) currants (8 oz/250 g)*

*1½ cups (375 mL) mixed peel (8 oz/250 g)*

*2 cups (500 mL) candied cherries (8 oz/250 g), halved*

*1¼ cups (300 mL) dried apricots, sliced (6 oz/175 g)*

*1 cup (250 mL) pitted prunes, sliced (6 oz/175 g)*

*1¼ cups (300 mL) chopped pecans (6 oz/175 g)*

*1½ cups (375 mL) all-purpose flour*

*1 tsp (5 mL) baking soda*

*¼ cup (50 mL) cocoa powder*

*½ cup (125 mL) butter, at room temperature*

*½ cup (125 mL) red currant, grape or raspberry jelly*

*1 cup (250 mL) granulated sugar*

*4 eggs*

*¼ cup (50 mL) rum or brandy*

*2 tbsp (25 mL) molasses*

*1 tsp (5 mL) ground ginger*

*1 tsp (5 mL) ground cinnamon*

*¼ tsp (1 mL) ground cloves*

*¼ tsp (1 mL) ground cardamom*

*About ½ cup (125 mL) rum or brandy (optional)*

*My* recipe-tester Heather Epp developed this recipe using lots of dried fruit, fruit jelly, cocoa and molasses. It is best if made at least six weeks before eating; during that time it should be wrapped in cheesecloth (or a clean J-cloth) that is soaked in rum or brandy and changed at intervals. Store it in a cool, dark place. Like good wine, this cake improves with age.

In large bowl, combine raisins, currants, mixed peel, cherries, apricots, prunes and pecans.

In small bowl, stir together flour and baking soda. Pour half over fruit; stir well to coat. Stir cocoa powder into remaining flour mixture.

In separate large bowl, using electric mixer, beat together butter and jelly until smooth. Add sugar, beating until fluffy. Add eggs, one at a time, beating well after each addition. Add rum, molasses, ginger, cinnamon, cloves and cardamom. Beat in flour mixture, scraping down sides of bowl, until smooth. Pour over fruit mixture; stir until combined. Pour batter into two 9 x 5-inch (2 L) loaf pans lined with buttered parchment or brown paper. Press with back of spoon to smooth top.

Bake in preheated 275 F (140 C) oven about 2½ hours or until tester inserted in centre comes out clean. Cool. Keep cake in paper liner. Pour 1 tbsp (15 mL) rum over loaves every week, if desired. Wrap in plastic wrap and foil. Store in cool place.

*Makes 2 loaves.*

# Light Fruitcake

My trusty recipe tester Heather Epp got this tried-and-true recipe from her aunt Edith. A lovely cake that would be great to keep on hand for any occasion.

*3 cups (750 mL) sultana raisins (1 lb/500 g)*

*2 cups (500 mL) candied cherries, halved (8 oz/250 g)*

*2 cups (500 mL) candied pineapple, cut in ½-inch (1 cm) pieces (8 oz/250 g)*

*1½ cups (375 mL) mixed peel (8 oz/250 g)*

*½ cup (125 mL) candied citron (3 oz/90 g)*

*1¼ cups (300 mL) chopped blanched almonds (4 oz/125 g)*

*1 cup (250 mL) shredded coconut (optional)*

*2¾ cups (675 mL) all-purpose flour*

*1 tsp (5 mL) baking powder*

*½ tsp (2 mL) grated nutmeg*

*1 cup (250 mL) butter, at room temperature*

*1 cup (250 mL) granulated sugar*

*3 eggs*

*1 tsp (5 mL) almond extract*

*½ tsp (2 mL) rose water (optional)*

*½ cup (125 mL) warm water*

*½ cup (125 mL) rum or brandy for aging (optional)*

In large bowl, combine raisins, cherries, pineapple, peel, citron, almonds and coconut (if using).

In small bowl, stir together flour, baking powder and nutmeg. Pour half over fruit and stir to coat each piece.

In separate large bowl, using electric mixer, cream butter and sugar until fluffy. Beat in eggs, one at a time, until smooth. Add almond extract and rose water (if using). Beat in remaining flour mixture alternately with warm water until batter is very smooth. Pour over fruit mixture. Stir, using wooden spoon, until thoroughly combined. Pour into 10-inch (3 L) springform pan or 10 x 6-inch (3 L) loaf pan lined with greased brown or parchment paper.

Bake in preheated 275 F (140 C) oven about 3 hours or until cake tester inserted in centre comes out clean. Cool. Keep cake in paper. Pour 2 tbsp (25 mL) rum over cake every week until serving, if desired. Wrap well in plastic wrap and foil and keep in cool place.

*Makes 1 large cake.*

# CHEATER'S FRUITCAKE

1 cup (250 mL) unblanched almonds (5 oz/150 g)

3 apples, peeled, cored and thinly sliced

¾ cup (175 mL) butter, at room temperature

1 cup (250 mL) packed brown sugar

4 eggs

3 cups (750 mL) all-purpose flour

2 tsp (10 mL) ground cinnamon

1 tsp (5 mL) baking soda

1 tsp (5 mL) ground ginger

1 tsp (5 mL) grated nutmeg

½ tsp (2 mL) salt

3 cups (750 mL) mincemeat

Icing sugar

Spread almonds in single layer on ungreased baking sheet. Toast in preheated 350 F (180 C) oven 10 minutes or until fragrant. Cool. Coarsely chop in food processor or by hand.

In bowl, combine almonds and apple slices.

In separate large bowl, cream butter and sugar until light. Beat in eggs, one at a time, scraping down sides occasionally.

In separate bowl, combine flour, cinnamon, baking soda, ginger, nutmeg and salt. Stir into butter mixture alternately with mincemeat until well combined. Stir in apple mixture. Pour into greased 10-inch (3 L) Bundt pan. Smooth top with spatula.

Bake in preheated 350 F (180 C) oven about 1½ hours or until cake tester inserted in centre comes out clean and cake bounces back when pressed with thumb. (If cake becomes too dark on top during baking, cover with foil.) Let cool in pan on rack. Turn out onto serving plate and dust with sifted icing sugar. Cake can be wrapped in brandy-soaked cheesecloth and stored in airtight container for up to 1 week, or be frozen for up to 3 months.

*Makes about 14 servings.*

*I* discovered the original version of this superb dessert (so moist and fruity, it tastes like a cross between a pudding and a cake) in *Homemaker's Magazine*. It's the creation of talented cook Jan Main, owner and instructor at Jan Main's Kitchen, a cooking school of long standing in Toronto's east end. Instead of running all over town to buy dried fruit, nuts and other key ingredients for traditional fruitcake, you just use a jar of storebought mincemeat. Apples contribute to the moist texture of this sensational cake. A word of warning: use the 10-inch (3 L) Bundt pan (the old-fashioned mould-shaped pan with sloping sides and a hole in the middle), or be prepared to adjust the baking times. Be careful not to undercook this cake; it should take the full baking time described here.

# CARROT PLUM PUDDING

*Toronto Star* recipe tester Karen Boulton gave me this recipe for a no-suet plum pudding many years ago. "About half the people in my family are vegetarians," says Boulton, "so we've been having this at Christmas dinner ever since I can remember." Douse it in brandy and serve flaming along with one of our delicious sauces. You can omit the eggs from this recipe with little change in the results.

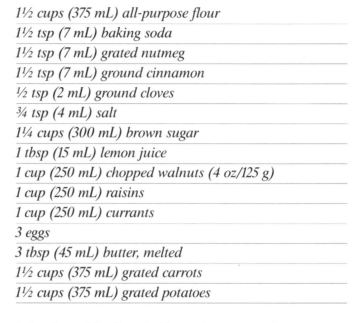

| |
|---|
| *1½ cups (375 mL) all-purpose flour* |
| *1½ tsp (7 mL) baking soda* |
| *1½ tsp (7 mL) grated nutmeg* |
| *1½ tsp (7 mL) ground cinnamon* |
| *½ tsp (2 mL) ground cloves* |
| *¾ tsp (4 mL) salt* |
| *1¼ cups (300 mL) brown sugar* |
| *1 tbsp (15 mL) lemon juice* |
| *1 cup (250 mL) chopped walnuts (4 oz/125 g)* |
| *1 cup (250 mL) raisins* |
| *1 cup (250 mL) currants* |
| *3 eggs* |
| *3 tbsp (45 mL) butter, melted* |
| *1½ cups (375 mL) grated carrots* |
| *1½ cups (375 mL) grated potatoes* |

In bowl, combine flour, baking soda, nutmeg, cinnamon, cloves, salt, sugar and lemon juice. Stir in walnuts, raisins and currants.

In separate large bowl, beat eggs. Gradually beat in melted butter. Using wooden spoon, stir in flour mixture just until moistened. Add carrots and potatoes. Mix well.

Pour into well-greased 6-cup (1.5 L) pudding mould or heat-proof bowl. Cover with double thickness of foil and secure with string. Place on rack in deep saucepan or preserving kettle with lid. Add boiling water to come halfway up side of bowl. Cover and steam over low heat 2 to 2½ hours or until cake tester inserted in centre comes out clean. Check water level occasionally and add boiling water if necessary.

Remove foil. Let pudding rest 10 minutes, then turn out onto rack. Cool completely. Wrap in plastic wrap, then foil. Refrigerate for up to 2 weeks, or freeze. To reheat, turn back into pudding mould or bowl and steam 1 hour or until heated through.

*Makes 12 servings.*

## Hard Sauce

This old-fashioned sauce is not for calorie-counters, but it is darned good. It quickly melts when you add it to the hot pudding. The sauce can be made two to three days ahead.

In bowl, beat ½ cup (125 mL) butter, at room temperature, until light. Add 2 cups (500 mL) icing sugar, 2 tbsp (25 mL) rum or brandy and 2 tbsp (25 mL) milk or cream. Beat until smooth. Pack into small serving dish and chill until firm. Sprinkle with grated nutmeg before serving.

*Makes about 1¾ cups (425 mL).*

## Yogurt Cheese Sauce

An absolutely delicious low-fat pudding sauce.

Place 3 cups (750 mL) low-fat plain yogurt in sieve lined with cheesecloth or clean tea towel. Place over bowl, cover and refrigerate 6 to 24 hours (yogurt will get thicker the longer it drains). Discard liquid or use it when baking breads or muffins.

In bowl, gently stir together thickened yogurt, 2 tbsp (25 mL) liquid honey, finely grated rind of 1 lemon and 2 tbsp (25 mL) Grand Marnier or orange liqueur (optional).

*Makes about 1¾ cups (425 mL).*

## Lemony Custard Sauce

In saucepan, combine ¼ cup (50 mL) granulated sugar and 2 tbsp (25 mL) cornstarch. Whisk in 1½ cups (375 mL) milk and place over medium-high heat. Cook, stirring constantly, about 10 minutes or until sauce comes to a boil.

Spoon small amount of hot sauce into 2 lightly beaten eggs to warm them, then whisk egg mixture into saucepan. Cook about 2 minutes or just until thickened. Remove from heat. Stir in 1 tsp (5 mL) vanilla and 1 tsp (5 mL) finely grated lemon rind. Transfer to bowl.

Place plastic wrap on surface of custard to prevent skin forming as custard cools. Serve warm.

*Makes 2 cups (500 mL).*

# FRUITCAKE COOKIES

*½ cup (125 mL) butter or margarine,*
*at room temperature*

*1 cup (250 mL) packed brown sugar*

*1 egg*

*1 cup (250 mL) all-purpose flour*

*½ tsp (2 mL) baking powder*

*¼ tsp (1 mL) salt*

*1½ cups (375 mL) crumbled fruitcake*

*1 cup (250 mL) rolled oats (not instant)*

In large bowl, cream butter and sugar until fluffy. Beat in egg until smooth.

In separate bowl, combine flour, baking powder and salt. Stir into butter mixture to form a soft dough. Stir in fruitcake and rolled oats. Mix well. Drop batter by heaping spoonfuls 2 inches (5 cm) apart on greased baking sheet.

Bake in preheated 350 F (180 C) oven 8 to 10 minutes or until golden-brown but still soft. Cool on racks.

*Makes 3 dozen cookies.*

## Fruitcake Truffles

Chop 2 cups (500 mL) crumbled light or dark fruitcake in food processor until it forms a ball. With dampened hands, form into 1-inch (2.5 cm) balls. Let stand on baking sheet lined with waxed paper, uncovered, 30 minutes.

Melt 1½ cups (375 mL) chopped bittersweet or semisweet chocolate in top of a double boiler or in microwave, stirring until smooth.

Place fruitcake balls on tines of fork and dip into melted chocolate, one at a time, letting excess drip off. Chill balls 30 minutes or until firm.

*Makes about 20 truffles.*

*A*s a fruitcake fan, I object to those jokes about festive fruitcake winding up as doorstops. However, should you be saddled with leftover cake (light or dark), it can be made into these super cookies from the *Use It Up Cookbook* by the helpful people at Glad. You could also try my Fruitcake Truffles – another imaginative way to recycle fruitcake. These cookies should keep about a week stored in an airtight container, or they can be frozen.

# GINGERBREAD COOKIES

*3¾ cups (925 mL) all-purpose flour*

*2 tsp (10 mL) ground cinnamon*

*2 tsp (10 mL) ground ginger*

*½ tsp (2 mL) baking soda*

*Pinch ground cloves*

*1 cup (250 mL) butter, at room temperature*

*1 cup (250 mL) brown sugar*

*1 cup (250 mL) molasses*

In bowl, combine flour, cinnamon, ginger, baking soda and cloves.

In large bowl, cream butter and sugar until fluffy. Beat in molasses until smooth. Gradually stir in flour mixture until soft dough is formed. Divide dough in two. Wrap in plastic wrap and refrigerate at least 1 hour or up to 3 days.

On floured surface, roll out dough to about ⅛-inch (.25 cm) thickness. Cut into desired shapes using floured cookie cutter. Place on lightly greased baking sheets.

Bake in preheated 350 F (180 C) oven about 7 minutes or until lightly browned at edges. Transfer cookies to wire racks. Cool completely before icing.

*Makes about 3 dozen cookies.*

## Royal Icing

In large bowl, beat 2 egg whites with electric mixer until frothy. Gradually add 3½ cups (875 mL) sifted icing sugar until all sugar is moistened. Increase speed to high and beat 5 to 7 minutes or until very stiff and shiny. Divide among small bowls and add food colouring as desired.

We developed these yummy cookies one Christmas, knowing that making gingerbread people is a favourite way for parents (those who have the time and patience!) to bake with their kids. These are thinner and crunchier than the cakier version of gingerbread cookies; I prefer them this way. Decorate them with Royal Icing, ideal for any festive cake or cookie.

# CHOCOLATE CHUNK SHORTBREAD

*2 cups (500 mL) butter, at room temperature*

*1 cup (250 mL) granulated sugar*

*3 cups (750 mL) all-purpose flour*

*1 cup (250 mL) rice flour*

*4 oz (125 g) bittersweet or semisweet chocolate, coarsely chopped*

*½ cup (125 mL) chopped pecans (2 oz/60 g), toasted*

In large bowl, cream butter and sugar until fluffy.

In separate bowl, combine all-purpose and rice flours. Gradually stir into butter mixture to form a crumbly dough. Stir in chocolate and pecans. Form a heaping tablespoonful of dough into a ball in palm of hand. Press thumb into centre slightly. Place on ungreased baking sheet about 1 inch (2.5 cm) apart. Place baking sheet in freezer at least 15 minutes.

Bake cookies in preheated 350 F (180 C) oven about 20 minutes or until lightly brown on bottom.

*Makes about 40 cookies.*

## Sidebar

*S*hortbread is one of my favourite festive foods. Rice flour, sold in supermarkets, is a key ingredient to this version and gives the cookies a melt-in-the-mouth quality. In this instance, counting cholesterol is out; you must use butter for the best flavour. Cutting the chocolate into chunks gives, I think, a better chocolate hit, but you could substitute chocolate chips, if desired.

# LIGHTENED EGGNOG

*6 eggs, separated*

*½ cup (125 mL) granulated sugar*

*4 cups (1 L) 1 percent milk*

*1 tsp (5 mL) vanilla*

*Cinnamon, nutmeg or chocolate*

In heavy saucepan, whisk together egg yolks and ¼ cup (50 mL) sugar. Stir in 2 cups (500 mL) milk. Cook over medium heat, stirring constantly, about 20 minutes or until custard coats back of spoon. Immediately pour into bowl; stir in remaining milk, vanilla and nutmeg. Chill at least 4 hours.

Just before serving, in large bowl, beat egg whites until frothy. Gradually add remaining ¼ cup (50 mL) sugar, beating until stiff peaks form. Slowly stir yolk mixture into egg whites to form a smooth drink. Serve in one large glass bowl garnished with cinnamon, nutmeg or chocolate, or in individual glasses.

*Makes 8 servings.*

## Sidebar

*A*n enlightened idea from the Ontario Egg Marketing Board, this is much lower in fat than the regular version and uses cooked instead of raw egg yolks, thus reducing the risk of bacteria. The recipe can easily be doubled for a crowd. For an alcoholic version, you could add ½ cup (125 mL) rum to the egg yolk mixture before folding in the egg whites.

# SUBSTITUTIONS IN A PINCH

*Here's a list of acceptable substitutions for those times when you're in a pinch. However, if an ingredient is key to the flavour of a recipe, it's best to wait until you have all the right stuff on hand.*

| If you don't have | Substitute |
|---|---|
| 1 tbsp (15 mL) chopped fresh herbs | 1 tsp (5 mL) dried |
| 1 tbsp (15 mL) herbes de provence | Combine 1 tsp (5 mL) thyme leaves + ½ tsp (2 mL) each marjoram leaves, oregano leaves, savory leaves and rosemary leaves |
| Fine herbs (*fines herbes*) | Equal amounts chervil, chives, tarragon and parsley |
| Pine nuts | Slivered almonds or chopped walnuts |
| Sake or rice wine | Dry white vermouth or dry sherry |
| Shallots | Finely chopped onion with half a finely chopped clove garlic |
| Chives | Green onions, including the tops, finely chopped |
| Molasses | Honey, maple syrup or dark corn syrup |
| 1 cup (250 mL) packed light brown sugar | ½ cup (125mL) dark brown sugar + ½ cup (125 mL) granulated sugar OR 1 cup (250 mL) granulated sugar + 1 tbsp (15 mL) molasses |
| 1 tsp (5 mL) baking powder | ¼ tsp (1 mL) baking soda + ½ tsp (2 mL) cream of tartar |
| 1 tsp (5 mL) ground allspice | ½ tsp (2 mL) ground cinnamon + ¼ tsp (1 mL) each grated nutmeg and ground cloves |
| Mace | Nutmeg |
| 1 tsp (5 mL) five-spice powder | Combine ½ tsp (2 mL) crushed anise seed star, ¼ tsp (1 mL) ground ginger, pinch each ground cinnamon and ground cloves |
| Superfine sugar | Granulated sugar processed in food processor until powdery |
| 1 cup (250 mL) cake and pastry flour | ¾ cup (175 mL) + 2 tbsp (25 mL) all-purpose flour |
| 1 cup (250 mL) self-rising flour | 1 cup (250 mL) all-purpose flour + 1½ tsp (7 mL) baking powder + ¼ tsp (1 mL) salt |
| 1 cup (250 mL) graham cracker crumbs | 13 graham crackers, ground in food processor OR 1 cup (250 mL) vanilla wafer crumbs |
| Dried currants | Chopped dark raisins |
| 1 oz (30 g) unsweetened chocolate | 3 tbsp (45 mL) unsweetened cocoa powder + 1 tbsp (15 mL) butter, shortening or vegetable oil |
| 1 cup (250 mL) milk | ½ cup (125 mL) evaporated milk + ½ cup (125 mL) water OR 1 cup (250 mL) water + ⅓ cup (75 mL) milk powder |
| 1 cup (250 mL) buttermilk | 1 tbsp (15 mL) lemon juice or white vinegar + enough milk to make 1 cup (250 mL) (let stand 5 minutes) |
| Sour cream | Plain yogurt |

# INDEX